M000235192

Jane Austen and the Fiction of Culture

to alexis —
i'm fucking dead.

Jane
Austen

THE ANTHROPOLOGY OF

FORM AND MEANING

Senior Editor

J. David Sapir (University of Virginia)

Associate Editors

Ellen B. Basso (University of Arizona)

J. Christopher Crocker (University of Virginia)

Hildred Geertz (Princeton University)

Peter A. Metcalf (University of Virginia)

Renato A. Rosaldo (Stanford University)

Jane Austen
and the Fiction of Culture
An Essay on the Narration of Social Realities

RICHARD HANDLER & DANIEL SEGAL

The University of Arizona Press   Tucson

The University of Arizona Press

Copyright © 1990
The Arizona Board of Regents
All Rights Reserved

This book was set in Fournier.
∞ This book is printed on acid-free, archival-quality paper.
Manufactured in the United States of America.

94 93 92 91 90   5 4 3 2 1

Library of Congress Cataloging-in-Publication Data
Handler, Richard, 1950–
Jane Austen and the fiction of culture: An essay on the narration of social
realities / Richard Handler and Daniel Segal.
    p.   cm. — (The Anthropology of form and meaning)
Includes bibliographical references.
ISBN 0-8165-1171-3 (alk. paper)
1. Austen, Jane, 1775–1817—Political and social views. 2. Social
history in literature. 3. Ethnology in literature. I. Segal,
Daniel Alan, 1958–   . II. Title. III. Series.
PR4038.P6H36   1990
823'.7—dc20   90-10866
CIP

British Library Cataloguing in Publication data are available.

FOR OUR PARENTS

Earl Handler, Phoebe Handler, Norman Segal,

and in memory of Bernice Ginsberg Segal

Contents

Acknowledgments

Both authors thank David Schneider. It was in his graduate seminar on kinship, in separate years, that each of us began working on Jane Austen as a social theorist and ethnographic writer. Moreover, it was he, along with George Stocking, who encouraged our collaboration. Jerrold Hogle, J. David Sapir, and Marilyn Strathern offered careful critical commentary on drafts of this book. Alma Gottlieb at the University of Illinois and Elizabeth Traube at the University of Chicago provided opportunities to present portions of this work before most attentive and helpful audiences. Finally, we thank Pitzer College for providing funds for a great many lengthy telephone calls over the last three years as we completed this work.

Some of the material presented here was previously published in the following essays: "Hierarchies of Choice: The Social Construction of Rank in Jane Austen," *American Ethnologist* 12:691–706 (1985); "Serious Play: Creative Dance and Dramatic Sensibility in Jane Austen, Ethnographer," *Man* 24:322–39 (1989); "Narrating Multiple Realities: Some Lessons from Jane Austen for Ethnographers," *Anthropology and Humanism Quarterly* 9(4):15–21 (1984).

Richard Handler acknowledges the late Meyer Fortes for his encouraging response to this research in its earliest moments. Clifford

Geertz also read an early version of R. H.'s Austen work and made suggestions for its development. Others who have been supportive of this project include Alison Booth, James Clifford, Gary Downey, Michael Ebner, Susan Fraiman, Dick Kuczkowski, Mia Leo, George Marcus, and Charles Miller.

Daniel Segal thanks Laurie Shrage for many provocative conversations on Jane Austen and feminist theory—and much more. While an undergraduate at Cornell University, D. S. had his interest in the interplay between anthropology and literature provoked and encouraged by Jim Boon. At the Claremont Colleges, Don Brenneis and Susan Seymour of Pitzer College provided a great deal of professional support (and many interesting conversations) while this and other projects were being completed; Ed Copeland of Pomona College generously shared his vast knowledge of Jane Austen.

Jane Austen and the Fiction of Culture

CHAPTER ONE

A World of Marriage

There was a young lady with certain connections, and she married.

There, in a single sentence, lies a tale, or more precisely at least six tales, for each of Jane Austen's novels concerns a young lady's movement from her natal family to the family created by her marriage. Moreover, in Austen's texts society is re-formed, though never made whole, by the picking of spouses and the fixing of matches. Thus the tales anticipate central concerns of twentieth-century anthropology, as more than a few of its practitioners have noted.

In this work we explore correspondences between Austen's texts and anthropological theories of kinship, social organization, and culture. We do so both as a means of reading Jane Austen and as a means of opening anthropological theory to alternative strategies of narration, interpretation, and translation. We examine both the social relations Austen narratively represented and her narrative means of representation. We use Austen's unceasing attention to the details of social life—her concern with such exotica as "cousins in love, &c." (*MP* 6)—to compare her fictions to anthropological studies of foreign tribes, and vice versa.[1] Our study of relations between

---

1. All quotations from Austen's novels are cited from *The Oxford Illustrated Jane Austen*, 3d ed. Ed. R. W. Chapman (London: Oxford University Press, 1932–

Austen and anthropology leads us into many thorny issues of text and context, narrative description and cultural translation, intertextuality and realism. However, we begin not with theory but in the field; that is, with an immersion in Austen's world of marriage. Our aim in adopting this ethnographic approach to Austen is not to evade theoretical reflexivity but to place it within an analysis of our primary data—Austen's six novels.

Austen's narratives engage her characters and readers alike in a common problem: the eventful, though conventional, process by which men and women make an exclusive and mutual choice of a partner. Like many ethnographers of 'exotic' societies, Austen focuses our attention on the rules of courtship and marriage. However, her understanding and depiction of social rules differs crucially from the positivist notion of behavioral norms that has dominated both anthropological theory and Jane Austen criticism, concerned, as it has been, with Austen's relationship to social order. In Austen's

----

69). Our text uses the following abbreviations to refer to the novels: *SS* for *Sense and Sensibility*, *PP* for *Pride and Prejudice*, *MP* for *Mansfield Park*, *E* for *Emma*, *NA* for *Northanger Abbey*, *P* for *Persuasion*, and *MW* for *Minor Works*. We provide page references in parentheses—for instance, (*NA* 110), or, if the title has been cited in the immediate passage, simply (110).

Throughout this book single quotation marks indicate a word or cultural concept from Austen's texts that is being set off for analysis; similarly, single quotation marks are used for anthropological and literary-critical concepts or terms we wish to examine without subscribing to their premises. We reserve double quotation marks for direct quotations.

For a provocative critique of Chapman's editing, see Claudia L. Johnson (1988: xvi–xvii), who argues that Chapman, unwilling to place Austen on a par with great *men* of letters, has used the ostensibly neutral language of textual scholarship to confine Austen to a world of *feminine* gentility: "With their appendixes detailing regency fashions in clothing, carriages, and modes of address, and their chronologies of events based on almanacs, Chapman's editions appear less to illuminate and to honor Austen's compositional process than to preserve the novels in a museumlike world situated somewhere between fiction and real life. As such, *The Oxford Illustrated Jane Austen* is a graceful monument to country life in regency England, a time which twentieth-century readers have been prone to idealize into graciousness and tranquility."

fiction of culture, we argue, social rules do not regulate the characters' conduct, nor do they ensure the reproduction of the established
social order; rather, they give significance and value to pragmatically pursued social action. As an initial illustration of this perspective we present seven of the meaningful principles that inform
marital choices in Austen's narrations.

1. Marriage produces offspring. In Austen's narrations it is axiomatic
that marriages are for sexual reproduction. Assumed by all, the point
is made explicit only in Emma's account of her determination to
remain single: "the want" of children, she notes, "is really the greatest evil to be avoided in *not* marrying" (*E* 86). In producing children,
marriages form "ties of blood" (*MP* 428)—that is, the presumably
natural bonds between parents and offspring and between siblings.

2. Marriage is a humanly constructed relationship. Though marriages
form ties of blood, they are nonetheless contrasted with natural ties.
Whereas people are born into a natal family, they enter into a marriage (*NA* 77). Marriage is thus not a given but a matter of choice.
For marital matches to be made, men and women must each select
and accept one of the other reciprocally.

3. Marital choices are exclusive. A marriage excludes other marriages, and a commitment to marry excludes other engagements. In
Sense and Sensibility Edward Ferrars regretfully avoids Elinor Dashwood because of his secret prior engagement to Lucy Steele. In *Pride
and Prejudice,* when Lady Catherine de Bourgh travels to Elizabeth
Bennet's home to state her objections to the rumored match between
Elizabeth and Mr. Darcy (Lady Catherine's nephew), she tells Elizabeth, "Mr. Darcy is engaged to *my daughter,*" and then asks, "Now
what have you to say?" Elizabeth responds: "Only this; that if he is
so, you can have no reason to suppose he will make an offer to me"
(*PP* 354). And in *Northanger Abbey* we get this additional evidence of
the exclusivity of marriage: "He looked as handsome and as lively as
ever, and was talking with interest to a fashionable and pleasing-
looking young woman, who leant on his arm, and whom Catherine
immediately guessed to be his sister; thus unthinkingly throwing
away a fair opportunity of considering him lost to her for ever, by
being married already" (*NA* 53). A person seeking the advantages
of marriage must try to find them in one unmarried person, not

in a person already married, and not in more than one person at once.

4. *Marriage is not a relation between siblings.* In *Mansfield Park* Mrs. Norris says that a marriage between people "brought up . . . like brothers and sisters" would be "morally impossible" (*MP* 6). In *Northanger Abbey* John Thorpe makes it clear that he considers his sisters distinct from potential romantic partners. Responding to the suggestion that he take one of his sisters for a ride in his carriage, he says, "I did not come to Bath to drive my sisters about, and look like a fool" (*NA* 99).

5. *Marriage should unite two people of the same social status.* Every potential marriage in the six novels is interpreted in terms of this general principle. *Persuasion* focuses on Anne Elliot, who lives in regret of having been "guided" to turn down a proposal from the man she loved because of his inferior status (*P* 29). *Northanger Abbey*, *Sense and Sensibility*, *Mansfield Park*, and *Pride and Prejudice* all end with the heroines' happy marriages to men who had been considered above them. Emma rejects the offer of Mr. Elton, a man she considers beneath her, and at the same time is mortified to see him reject Harriet Smith, her protégée, on the grounds that Harriet is his inferior. In all these cases those in favor of a proposed marriage claim that it will unite parties of equal status, while those opposed to it perceive inequality. The confrontation between Lady Catherine de Bourgh and Elizabeth Bennet mentioned above shows the possibility of divergent opinions concerning the status endogamy of any match. Lady Catherine tells Elizabeth, "If you were sensible of your own good, you would not wish to quit the sphere, in which you have been brought up." Elizabeth responds not by rejecting the principle of status endogamy but by offering an alternative view of the relative status of the parties involved: "In marrying your nephew, I should not consider myself as quitting that sphere. He is a gentleman; I am a gentleman's daughter; so far we are equal" (*PP* 356).

6. *Marriage should bring advantage.* Early in *Mansfield Park* Mary Crawford declares that "every body should marry as soon as they can do it to advantage" (*MP* 43). In *Pride and Prejudice* Charlotte Lucas accepts Mr. Collins on the basis of a few days' acquaintance because it is a profitable match. Mary Crawford resists a marriage with Edmund

Bertram because Edmund, as Sir Thomas Bertram's second son, will be comfortable but not wealthy. In *Northanger Abbey* Isabella Thorpe switches her attachment from James Morland to Frederick Tilney, who has both great wealth and great rank, after she learns of the modest financial arrangements proposed by Morland's father. *Sense and Sensibility* and *Pride and Prejudice* both contain philandering young men who seek to attach themselves to wealthy women. The seeking of advantage in marriage leads, in practice, to conflicts with the ideal of status endogamy, as well as with the next feature.

7. Marriage should be based on symmetrical romantic attraction. In Austen's narrations every marriage made solely for advantage is criticized by those outside the marriage as lacking romance, that is, the experience of mutual attraction based on personal taste rather than on such public tokens of worth as money and status. The concept of romance helps us see a distinction made in the Austen texts between a personal domain and a public one, and it is because of this distinction that many characters see romance and advantage as exclusive opposites. For example, Marianne Dashwood is known to other characters in *Sense and Sensibility* for her objection to "second attachments" (*SS* 55) and, more generally, to any relationship not based on an immediate and overwhelming experience of love. By contrast, she says that though "the world would be satisfied" by a marriage of "convenience, . . . [in] my eyes it would be no marriage at all. . . . To me it would seem only a commercial exchange, in which each wished to be benefited at the expense of the other" (*SS* 38). Because romantic attraction does not necessarily accord with a calculated estimation of wealth and rank, characters often find it difficult to balance considerations of romance with considerations of status equality and advantage.

This preliminary discussion has led us to locate marriage in a larger discourse involving family ties and incest, nature and selection, social rank and exchange. In recognizing that marriage involves exclusive selection, we have suggested that it is understood as a humanly constructed relationship. By contrast, natural relations are established by ties of blood, and are not subject to choice or selection. In courtship the selectivity of marriage is epitomized by exclusivity; it is a choice in the most extreme sense because it eliminates alternatives. Yet the exclusivity of marriage contains a complementary meaning as well, for it also represents permanence: a marriage cannot easily be replaced. And the permanence of marriage expresses the role of marriage in producing, in the next generation, ties of blood, which are conceived of as naturally fixed. The taboo against incest emphatically asserts the contrast between natural relationships, or family ties, and selected relationships, or connections. Incest is morally impossible and unnatural because it conflates marriage connections and family ties, for it uses a natural tie to build a selected relationship.

Yet the marked contrast between family ties and marital connections—represented by the taboo on incest—does not exhaust the meaningful relations between the two terms. Marital partners should be from different families, but a marital connection must be like a person's natal family ties in at least two ways. First, marital partners should be as compatible as persons naturally alike and attached. Second, marital relations should, at a minimum, maintain the status of a person's natal family. Thus both romance and considerations of rank affirm a principle of endogamy that makes the bonds of matrimony like the ties of blood. Yet at the same time both also affirm a principle of exogamy, specifically a principle of hypergamy: romantically, one should marry a person one esteems, and practically, a person of higher status.

So far, then, we have sketched a series of terms—*marriage, family,* and *incest*—and we have suggested that they are related in terms of two principles of discrimination: (1) a distinction between what is natural and what is selected, and (2) a distinction between propriety, in the sense of what is consistent with or an improvement on nature, and transgressions of nature. We can sum up these comments with the table below.

We have begun by offering a sampling of an analysis of the implicit cultural principles of Austen's emplotted discourse on marriage, courtship, rank, and gender. We develop this analysis further throughout the first half of this book. Thereafter we consider how Austen's narratives allow readers as distant as ourselves an entrance into a partially foreign, partially familiar social world. In brief, we

TABLE I. *Principles of Discrimination for Marriage, Family, and Incest*

	Family	Marriage	Incest
selected (+)/given (−)	−	+	+/−
proper (+)/improper (−)	+	+	−

treat Austen's novels first as texts to be interpreted and second as exemplars of both intercultural translation and intracultural de-familiarization. Throughout the development of this double image of Austen's texts we seek to demonstrate that her fiction can help us establish the fictiveness of social realities.

Following a broad tradition of cultural analysis, we begin with the premise that the meaning of human acts can be understood by others because these acts are patterned or structured. Moreover, this patterning of human experience is, in Saussure's terms, naturally arbitrary, that is, fundamentally social: it is learned from others and changed through its use in meaningful, communicative interactions. We introduced this work by proposing an interpretation of the meaningful principles that organize the characters' discourse of marriage, and we go on to examine their understanding and practice of kinship, courtship, and social status (or rank). We do not, however, present our interpretation as a model of a singular, bounded sociocultural system ("the English gentry circa 1800"). We challenge the search for such singular social totalities—though not for patterning or structure—on two closely related grounds, and though we discuss these intermittently, they are outlined here because they are fundamental tenets of our interpretive approach.

First, we argue that cultural principles necessarily contain unrealized alternatives. Cultural principles are established by opposition—between romantic partners and siblings, men and women, natural ties and humanly created relations, and so on—and a logic of opposition can always be operated on such distinctions themselves. The distinction between romantic partners and siblings can, for instance, be blurred or further fragmented, and in various ways. Because of the generative power of negative dialectics, we reject the Saussurian division of language into uniformly shared principles (*langue*) and diverse, variable communicative acts (*parole*). Rather, we identify variation as an inherent possibility of all meaningful principles, and we argue that communicative acts can, at least potentially, create alternative principles of social action and relations. If *parole* exhibits daily variation, it can only be because *langue* itself is inherently mutable. In sum, we blur the boundaries of Saussure's famous opposition.

Second, we challenge the conception of an integrated cultural system in terms of the contingency of the boundaries of such systems.[2] Human beings are not, we argue, organized into discrete social totalities whose members share a singular and distinct culture; communication occurs, after all, across all social boundaries, and boundaries themselves are communicative signs. Because we see social groups as precipitates of social action that are formed and dissolved in particular contexts, we reject attempts to identify Austen's texts with a singular social context, or society. For us, the problem of using her works is one of a multitude of intertextual relations: between the words of different characters, between her narrative structures and plots, between one novel and another within her oeuvre, between Austen's writings and texts about and by her contemporaries, and between her novels and various ethnological inscriptions.

Critics of the position taken here might argue that the failure to assume the existence of a bounded cultural system would preclude scientific inquiry by introducing inexhaustible complexity into cultural analyses. We would respond that the variability of cultural principles may make cultural analysis open-ended, but it is also what makes cultural analysis possible: if a culture had a fixed and invariant set of arbitrary principles, it could not be translated into any other. People can communicate across cultures because any culture can be transformed—conceptually and communicatively—into any other.

The seven principles of marriage with which we began can be seen as the product of just such a communication across cultures.

---

2. Each author has developed this argument in separate work; cf. Handler (1988) and Segal (1988).

Because Jane Austen's world is at once familiar to and distant from late-twentieth-century English-speaking readers, these principles, taken as a set, may seem both obvious and strange. To stress, for example, that marriage produces offspring, and to claim for such a statement the status of an interpretive principle of Jane Austen's world, might seem a belaboring of the obvious. Yet such emphasis constitutes a strategy of defamiliarization that is central to our interpretive approach, and, we claim, intimately related to Jane Austen's. When anthropologists study an exotic culture, their immediate task is to make sense of seemingly senseless practices: the strange must be made familiar. By contrast, when studying familiar cultures, the task is one of defamiliarization: the familiar must be made strange. These two tasks belong to a single interpretive project, anthropology's version of the hermeneutic spiral. To develop an understanding of the strange, one must call into question one's own commonsense categories (else one will read them into the common sense of others), and one of the most effective methods to develop an estranged understanding of the familiar is to rethink common sense from the perspective of the exotic.

Our initial discussion of principles of marriage in Austen emerged for us by relating her texts to an ethnographic literature that tells of marriage systems constructed on the basis of quite different principles. For example, the apparently obvious notion that marriage is an exclusive relationship between one man and one woman becomes newly significant when we compare it to the ideas of Mormons who are polygynous, Tibetans who are polyandrous, or the Kwakiutl of British Columbia, who understand such marital alternatives as feet and halves of a body (Boas 1966: 55). Were we to place the Austen texts in still another comparative sphere, we could ask what they say about marriages with animals. Or, to pick an example more pertinent to our contemporary readers, we might ask about the meaning of the texts' uniform presupposition that marriage is a heterosexual relationship by comparing it to a conception that marriages can be homosexual.[3]

---

3. From a contemporary American viewpoint, the question of homosexuality seems reasonable, though not so the question of bestiality. For Queen Victoria, or so the anecdote goes, male homosexuality was a thinkable and objectionable

Each of these comparative points of reference can enable readers to gain uniquely distanced interpretive leverage with respect to Austen's texts, which in turn allows us to construct a reading of the meaning of her tales of marriage. But comparative perspectives can be generated imaginatively, out of various sorts of 'thought experiments,' as well as out of the constructions of culturally distanced others. For example, the great sociologist Max Weber developed a method of social analysis based on the ideal type—a logically constructed model against which the messier phenomena described by the analyst's data could be compared. Weber explicitly argued that the social formation represented by the ideal type—for example, pure-market rationality or charismatic authority—was not to be encountered in the phenomenal world; rather, the model was useful precisely because it gave the analyst an imaginative perspective against which to interpret sociological and historical data.

For us, the novels of Jane Austen represent yet a third form of the comparativist imagination. As we will argue at length in the chapters that follow, Austen does not describe, defend, or even criticize a unified moral order. Rather, she denatures (that is, encultures) common sense by creating characters and voices with differing perspectives on, and interpretations of, commonsense meanings and morality. Austen's narrative techniques privilege multiplicity rather than unity; they create conversations, negotiations, and confrontations in which any voice or perspective can call into question the completeness of any other. Of these narrative techniques, Austen's use of irony is the most frequently discussed, and we will have occasion to comment on it. Other features of Austen's work that facilitate comparativist social analysis range from the telescoped endings of her plots to what we term the 'alter-cultural' communicative acts of her heroines' courtships.

---

possibility requiring legal sanctions, but lesbianism was so impossible that there was no need for man-made laws against it. Whereas the Kwakiutl marry their feet, others give them funerals: "Gen. Antonio Lopez de Santana, three times dictator of Mexico, held a magnificent funeral for the right leg he had lost in the so-called Pastry War" (García Márquez 1983: 4).

Our formulation of the conceptual principles informing courtship and marriage in Austen's texts stems both from anthropological comparisons external to the text and from Austen's depiction of variations within what has too frequently been seen as a unified social order. From our perspective, Austen never simply presupposes social norms or reproduces a static system of etiquette. Indeed, in Austen's fiction of culture the mere articulation of a principle of propriety by a character is an indication that the principle is open to some dispute, or at least doubt, by at least some characters, if only the metacharacter, the narrative voice. If there were no doubt about the principle or its correct interpretation, then the principle would be unlikely to be at issue in conversation, or on someone's mind in moments of reflection. Because Austen's texts generate voices that question apparently unquestioned (and unquestionable) cultural rules, she teaches us that such rules are not determinative but fictive, not natural objects but creations made and remade by people.

Our anthropological dialogue with Jane Austen can be related to debates in literary criticism on her work. These have focused largely on the relationship of Austen to the social order she inscribed and lived within. Some have considered her an appreciative chronicler, and conservative defender, of the moral order of a functionally integrated, traditional society. In a related vein, other critics have seen Austen as a reformer seeking the removal of corruption from a social order to which she was ultimately committed. Both readings envision a well-ordered society which they locate in the past, and both groups ground this social utopia in a universal nature and reason whose absence in the present they decry.[4] By contrast, others

4. One of the most curious arguments that proponents of the conservative reading make is that Austen defended the true meanings of words. Stuart Tave, for example, claims that Austen equates the proper use of language with a correct naming of reality: "There is a definable reality, not to be made or unmade, to which Jane Austen's men and women must bring themselves. . . . Like Jane Austen herself, admirable characters in her novels dislike hearing dislocated words that do not meet the reality" (1973: 18–19; cf. Tanner 1986: 6). Austen's sensitivity to the contextual dynamics of words is examined below, specifically in our discussion of 'family' and 'connections' in chapter 3.

have found a subversive Austen who undermines tradition with her well-documented repertoire of wit and irony. Like conservative readings of Austen, subversive accounts presuppose a highly structured society of a time now past, but argue that its ascribed hierarchies and enforced etiquette went against, rather than with, reason and human nature. These subversive readings of Austen have been extended in recent feminist scholarship, which sees the traditional order as an order of gender and class domination, and seeks in Austen liberatory opposition to it. Our approach joins these feminist readings in arguing that Austen's fiction depicts the mutual shaping of domestic and class hierarchies. Yet most feminist readings have, in our view, failed to articulate adequately the capacity of Austen's narratives to establish the contingency, and hence the alterability, of her gendered, classed order. Throughout the range of Austen criticism, then, readers have located her works in the context of a social order rigidly determined by inviolable behavioral rules. This well-ordered world is celebrated by some and deplored by others, but most share what we term a mechanistic or deterministic theory of society and social action. Thus, ironically, literary critics, who more than other scholars might be expected to focus on the interpretive play of social life, have failed to do so.

The conservative reading of Austen has recently been renewed by Marilyn Butler, who does us the service of placing Austen's work in the context of the "war of ideas" fomented by sentimentalism, romanticism, the French Revolution, and the conservative reaction to all of these. For Butler, "Jane Austen is conservative in a sense no longer current. Her morality is preconceived and inflexible. She is firm in identifying error, and less interested than other great novelists in that type of perception for which the novel is so peculiarly well adapted—the perception that thoroughly to understand a character is to forgive him" (1975: 298). Butler's insistence on Austen's straightforward conservatism presents her with difficult problems in interpreting the ironies, omissions, and partial truths that the novelist builds into her heroines' perspectives and musings. Butler even suggests that the novel is "a form made to convey moral relativism" (31), but, by the terms of her own argument, such a form must be inadequate to Jane Austen's conservative intentions. Butler resolves this difficulty by finding technical flaws in Austen's novels precisely at those points where Austen's achievements seem to defy Butler's interpretation (213–18, 245–49).

In contrast to Butler's uncompromising reading, Tony Tanner sees Austen as a reformer committed to a traditional social order but unwilling to countenance the moral failings of the upper classes responsible for maintaining that order: "If in *some* ways Jane Austen's vision is complicit with the dominant ideology of her class, in other ways it very clearly transcends it—for by how few of her characters taken from that class is she or her writing deceived, or 'taken in'!" (1986: 6). Tanner goes on to argue that Austen's criticism of "a sick society" (285)—a hierarchical world of landed wealth disrupted by the more liquid wealth of emergent industrial capitalism—led her to defend propriety stringently and to censure those of her characters who failed to uphold its standards. As Tanner puts it, property without propriety "could prove helpless to prevent a possible revolution in society. . . . This is one reason why Jane Austen constantly sought to establish and demonstrate what was the necessary proper conduct in all areas of social behaviour, why she scrutinised so carefully any possible deviance from, or neglect of, true propriety" (18).

With its attention to Austen as reformer, a reading like Tanner's—or the similar one of Alistair Duckworth (1971: 23–24)—can perhaps be seen as mediating between the vision of Austen as conservative and the subversive reading of an Austen in revolt against the constraints of hypocritical social conventions. Subversive readings tend to be linked explicitly to social-scientific theories, whether psychological, materialist, or feminist. For example, recoiling from the Janeites, D. W. Harding wrote a celebrated essay on "regulated hatred" in Austen's novels that espouses the view that Austen was not "a delicate satirist." Rather, her novels represented an outlet for a keenly critical intelligence that both depended on and was repelled by genteel society: "Her object is not missionary; it is the more desperate one of merely finding some mode of existence for her critical attitudes" (1940: 42, 46). Harding's reading is psychological and reductionist, and he was followed in this approach by Marvin Mudrick, who thoroughly explored Austen's use of irony, which he interpreted as a psychological defense on the part of the author against "the ultimate commitment of sex" (1952: 30, 194). Like Harding, Mudrick dwells on Austen's ambivalence, seeing her not as a visionary social critic but as a sometime renegade from the social order to which she was at other times committed: "Her alternation between defiance and submission toward it [her society]— that is, between an ironic and a conventional view of her materials—is the central fact" (263).

Other subversive readings focus on Austen's response to economic oppression and patriarchy. Mark Schorer and Dorothy Van Ghent both see Austen as exploring the discrepancy between the appearance of civility and the underlying reality of economic necessity, or, in Schorer's terms, "between social sentiment and social fact" (1952: 84). For Van Ghent, the issue is the dependency of women: "The tale [*Pride and Prejudice*] is that of a manhunt, with the female the pursuer and the male a shy and elusive prey. The desperation of the hunt is the desperation of economic survival: girls . . . must succeed in running down solvent young men in order to survive" (1953: 101).

Feminist readings have been greatly elaborated in the last ten years, particularly in the work of such critics as Judith Lowder Newton (1981), Margaret Kirkham (1983), Mary Poovey (1984), Daniel Cottom (1985), Nancy Armstrong (1987), and Claudia Johnson (1988). Because they are particularly concerned with the emergence of women writers, they have discussed the uses of fiction to liberate voices otherwise suppressed. But as social theorists, they have, for the most part, imagined the oppressiveness of Austen's society in deterministic terms. Moreover, in reading Austen they have sought and valorized prescience of late-twentieth-century strategies for liberation, thereby suggesting that these strategies are not located in our own historical experience but instead are transhistorical universals. This, in effect, places both Austen and ourselves out of context, and, ironically, joins conservatives in subscribing to a vision of a social order grounded in universal reason rather than particular histories.[5]

---

5. For a critique of universalist tendencies in recent feminist scholarship see Shrage (1989). On the problematics of presentist views of feminist politics see Cott's careful historicization of the feminist movement (1987).

This universalist tendency in recent feminist readings emerges even in those critics who seek a contextualized reading of Austen. For example, Newton begins her examination of various subversive strategies in Austen by retrieving an earlier definition of power that, she argues, is more appropriate to Austen than current conceptions of power as political domination. According to Newton, Austen explored women's power not as dominance and control but as "achievement and competence and, by implication as a form of self-definition or self-rule" (1981: 7). In accordance with this definition, Newton sees Elizabeth Bennet as empowered by her extraordinary wit and vivacity. Yet, ultimately, Newton deems this power a fantasy because of its inability to affect the brute facts of political and economic domination. For Newton, Elizabeth's acceptance of Darcy does not illuminate the contingency of rank and gender (see chapter 4, below) but is a personal "decline" misrepresented by Austen as a success in order "to preserve the fantasy of Elizabeth's power" (81). Implicitly, then, Newton's critique of Austen's mystification demands of Austen either an anachronistic program for radical change or a frank admission of an incapacity to overcome oppression.

While we agree with Newton (and other feminist critics) that Austen's narratives probe the constraints and conventions of a patriarchal order, we contest the characterization of Austen as ultimately caught by this order of domination. Austen's vision, we argue in this book, is not so much for or against the established social order as it is against any and all notions of a naturally grounded social order, whether a conservative vision of the nature of tradition or a radical vision of a utopian future. Her semiotic, rather than deterministic, view of cultural principles is of a piece with her insistence that the institutions of any society be understood as arbitrary, contingent, and subject to reinterpretation. No social order, her narratives suggest, should be rendered as natural, and all should be subject to what we term alter-cultural, serious play. Austen does not acquiesce to the gendered and classed social order she describes; rather, she instantiates how persons with various degrees of independence within it might render it otherwise.

The theoretical orientation that we have introduced here is embodied in the organization of the work that follows. To begin, we have constructed a model of the distinctions, categories, and conceptual associations commonly understood by the characters within Austen's novels (chapters 1, 2, and 3). To do this we have grouped the characters from different novels together as part of one set.[6] This contextualization of the six novels provides an effective basis for understanding both the differences of perspective found within them and the conflicting opinions of such contemporaries of Austen as Mary Wollstonecraft and Edmund Burke (chapter 9). In constructing an interpretation of the conceptual principles commonly comprehended by the characters in Austen's texts, we deal both with principles of etiquette that the characters themselves label conventional wisdom and implicit principles that we render visible by anthropological comparisons external to the texts.

Following our study of the characters' mutually comprehended cultural principles, we proceed to another aggregate analysis, this time of behavior (chapters 4, 5, and 6). By comparing the actions of the characters to their ideals and cultural premises, we emphasize how the characters creatively negotiate conventional wisdom to enact, maintain, and change their social relations. In this portion of the analysis we focus primarily, though not exclusively, on the relationship of status and rank to courtship and marriage in Austen's texts.

In addition, we contrast our twofold aggregate interpretations of Austen's fictional world to the particular histories of the heroines and their eventual spouses (chapters 5, 6, and 7). We argue that their tales are neither conventional nor antisocial, but alter-cultural. These characters avoid both facile acceptance and facile rejection of conventional etiquette and propriety. They recognize and understand social conventions not as rules that limit their behavior but as meaningful principles with which to communicate—playfully and

6. Thus the present work differs from much critical writing on Austen in not being subdivided into units, such as the chapters of book-length studies, that reproduce what is apparently taken to be a natural subdivision of Austen's oeuvre into six novels. (In this scheme the *Juvenilia* and other minor works sometimes provide further units.)

seriously but never literally or normatively. In this third moment of the analysis, then, we examine how the heroines and their partners richly communicate through interactions that comment on—and thereby displace—conventional etiquette and propriety.

Finally, we examine similarly self-conscious metacommentary, expressed through the narrative voices and plot structure, that establishes the potential for rich communication between text and readers (chapters 7, 8, and 9). In simplest terms, the mere presence of two opinions about what, for instance, constitutes a good match suggests a comment about both opinions—most obviously, to borrow Austen's happy phrase, that neither one is "universally acknowledged." As a result of the interaction between different points of view, we can read metacommentary about different interpretive logics, precisely because there are differences, as well as similarities. At some points in Austen's texts this metacommentary has an immediate presence—for instance, when a narrator emerges from the narration and addresses the reader directly. At other times this metacommentary is quite distant—for instance, when the narrative presents the reader with two equally coherent, but irreconcilable, accounts of the same incident. Thus Austen's texts move back and forth, occasionally making an explicit comment on different interpretive logics, and continuously, though implicitly, allowing (asking?) the reader to do so as well. We have noted that diversity within the novels, and distance between the reader and the texts, prevent any definitive interpretation of Austen's fictions, but now we can add that a definitive interpretation must be precluded because diversity and distance allow for an inexhaustible multiplicity of interpretations, each of which comments on the others. Thus the lack of a definitive interpretation is not really a lack but the source of the novels' strength. We can learn the subtleties of a range of understandings of experience from Austen's texts precisely because they are made up of the lively interaction of many differentiated points of view, and because no single point of view is allowed to obliterate others.

The Natural, the Civil, and the Unnatural

For Austen's characters, the contrast between family, marriage, and incest is one instance of a more general contrast between the natural, the civil, and the unnatural. *Nature* refers to what is given to humans—to the essences of things and to consequences that occur by necessity. Human actions either harmoniously enhance or dysfunctionally violate nature. Nature and the correlative terms of human action are central to Austen's plots about kinship, courtship, and marriage. These mutually constituting terms are largely givens for Austen's characters; that is to say, nature and its associated oppositions are themselves naturalized. Austen's narratives, by contrast, present a sustained perception of the social ontology of nature, and thus of its meaningfulness. By setting differing perceptions of nature into dialogic relief, Austen's narratives show us that nature is grounded in a contingent, and hence alterable, cultural base.

Moreover, beyond questions of kinship, courtship, marriage, motivation, and necessity, the category *nature* is, for Austen, deeply implicated in epistemological questions of truth, knowledge, and representation. To anticipate themes that will be developed in subsequent chapters, Austen's defamiliarization of nature is one facet of a more general critique of empiricism—that is, the sensibility of knowledge. Austen's texts undercut the conviction that nature, truth, and reality can be known without the mediation of interpretive schemes. Thus the most significant issues in cultural theory raised by Austen's oeuvre are intimately related to her ethnography of nature in her characters' social lives, and in particular her ethnography of kinship (cf. Cottom 1985: 112–13).

One of the least frequent but most telling uses of the term *nature* occurs when characters speak of nature as a model or guide for human art, artifice, and judgment. Consider, for instance, its use in this moment of reconciliation between Emma and Mr. Knightley, following a quarrel over Emma's attempts at matchmaking:

> . . . she could not help saying, as he was admiring the baby,
>
> "What a comfort it is, that we think alike about our nephews and nieces. As to men and women, our opinions are sometimes very different; but with regard to these children, I observe we never disagree."
>
> "If you were as much guided by nature in your estimate of men and women, and as little under the power of fancy and whim in your dealings with them, as you are where these children are concerned, we might always think alike." (*E* 98–99)

In this passage, to be "guided by nature" in one's judgment is to assess reality correctly. Thus Mr. Knightley's recourse to nature in the context of an ongoing quarrel is a rhetorically powerful ploy that Emma resists: "'To be sure—our discordancies must always arise from my being in the wrong.' 'Yes,' said he, smiling—'and reason good. I was sixteen years old when you were born.'" The entire conversation is rendered with a sustained irony. Though Mr. Knightley's judgments are often shown to be apter than Emma's, a reading of the entire novel shows that he is by no means infallible. His claim to superior wisdom not only grounded in, but quantified in terms of, a natural difference in age is precisely the sort of claim that Austen's narrations examine and undercut. Her characters may use the term *nature* to refer to reality, or to privilege assessments of reality—but Austen's novels consistently question such interpretive stances.

If, for Austen's characters, nature is a given, it is also said to give, to endow human beings with various attributes. People are said to have been endowed by nature with specific innate qualities. There are natural talents and virtues as well as natural defects. Captain Wentworth is characterized by "natural grace" (*P* 68), and Lucy Steele is said to be "naturally clever" (*SS* 127). Edward Ferrars has "natural shyness" (*SS* 15), and Charles Bingley "natural modesty" (*PP* 199). In general, any person can be said to have a specific nature, by which it is meant that some combination of personal traits, or a general attitude or temperament, is innate in him or her. Particular persons are described as good-natured or ill-natured, or as having an excellent, a tender, a modest, or a cruel nature. There are discussions of man's nature as opposed to woman's nature (*P* 232–33), and of human nature in general.

Though certain qualities and characteristics of human beings are natural, humans are not necessarily limited to being solely what they naturally are. On the contrary, improvement is both a practical and a moral imperative. What is given to human beings in or by nature must be added to or improved by human means—in particular by the exercise of human reason through proper choice. Education and society assist this process by working on innate potential (*PP* 70), developing and refining it to produce the polished attributes of mind and manner that characterize gentility. Moreover, improvement resulting from education is considered essential to the formation of a civilized adult. Few natural talents are usable without cultivation or training, whereas most natural deficiencies can be overcome or offset by education. Thus Henry Crawford, though "not handsome," has such a "pleasing address" that the Bertram sisters find him "the most agreeable young man" of their acquaintance (*MP* 44). On the other hand, natural talents without training remain mere potential, unavailable or undeveloped for the purposes of social interaction. Fanny Price's discovery of her sister Susan when she visits her home at Portsmouth illustrates this belief. Fanny is at first shocked by the "determined character" of Susan's manners—at her rudeness, in fact. But she gradually comes to admire Susan, for she realizes that Susan, without the benefit of education, sees what is right and tries, however unsuccessfully, to act accordingly: "Susan saw that much was wrong at home, and wanted to set it right. That a girl of fourteen, acting only on her own unassisted reason, should err in the method of reform was not wonderful [i.e., surprising]; and Fanny soon became more disposed to admire the natural light of the mind which could so early distinguish justly, than to censure severely the faults of conduct to which it led" (*MP* 395). It falls to Fanny, then, to educate Susan, and timid as Fanny has always been, "she did resolve to give occasional hints to Susan, and endeavor to exercise for her advantage the juster notions of what was due to every body, and what would be wisest for herself, which her own more favoured education had fixed in her" (*MP* 396). In sum, Fanny's assessment of Susan shows belief in both the naturalness of intelligence and moral sense and the necessity of education to develop and fix them for social purposes.

In addition to the personal qualities of human beings, aspects and attributes of the nonhuman natural world can be improved by human action. For example, the "natural taste" of Mrs. Grant's apricots is said to benefit from the "assistance" of her cook (*MP* 54). But it is with respect to their landed estates that Jane Austen's gentry demonstrate their greatest interest in improvement. The improvements at Sotherton, Everingham, and Thornton Lacey are important topics of discussion in *Mansfield Park,* and improvement is also an issue for John Dashwood (*SS* 225) and George Knightley (*E* 100–107). Mr. Darcy's Pemberley gives us the best example of what an improved estate ought to be:

> It was a large, handsome, stone building, standing well on rising ground, and backed by a ridge of high woody hills;—and in front, a stream of some natural importance was swelled into greater, but without any artificial appearance. Its banks were neither formal, nor falsely adorned. Elizabeth was delighted. She had never seen a place for which nature had done more, or where natural beauty had been so little counteracted by an awkward taste. (*PP* 245)

Here natural beauty has been improved by human ingenuity. The weight of the passage suggests that improvement results only when the potential of the unimproved scene is developed. "Awkward taste" too often counteracts "natural beauty," adding what is formal, artificial, and falsely adorned (cf. Duckworth 1971: 38–55; Van Ghent 1953: 107–8).

The example of Pemberley shows that the improvement of nature must follow nature itself, or else improvement misfires and creates the unnatural. In other words, human reason—itself a part of nature—must follow the dictates of nature in order to improve and thereby create civil society. In civil society, then, human beings have transcended nature, but without violating natural principles or laws.[1] And civil society is, in both a pragmatic and a moral sense, the proper state of human life. When Mrs. Elton plans a party to gather strawberries, she envisions an outdoor table—"every thing as natural and simple as possible." But Mr. Knightly counters her proposal by saying, "My idea of the simple and the natural will be to have the table spread in the dining-room. The nature and the simplicity of gentlemen and ladies, with their servants and furniture, I think is best observed by meals within doors" (*E* 355). In other words, Mr. Knightley discriminates between what in other narratives are called "human nature in a civilized state" (*NA* 109) and human nature "in a state of utter barbarism" (*MP* 441). What is natural for human beings, in Mr. Knightley's view, is that which has been selected by human reason in accordance with nature itself. People who attempt to deny that there is a properly civilized nature for human beings act unnaturally, though they may think that they can return to a nature that is at once prehuman and appropriate for humans. In sum, the attempt to recapture a presocialized nature is a bad choice, hence unnatural. Similarly, the renunciation of selection, the choice to remain in a presocialized natural state, is all *too* natural—that is, it is really a selection of the natural, and thus un-

1. Our argument at this point has been influenced by David Schneider's analysis of related themes in mid-twentieth-century American culture. Schneider notes that in the American conception of an "ideal" family, "there is the mastery of nature through nature's own laws, humanly selected and intelligently ordered." The ideal family is one manifestation of a more generally applicable ideal, according to which human reason "at once distinguishes the human from the animal, yet keeps [social institutions] all within the realm of nature and based on nature" (1968: 109–10).

natural and immoral. The phrase "all too natural" is used to describe the relationship of Lydia and Wickham in *Pride and Prejudice* (279), a relationship based primarily on sexuality. In this case an excessive indulgence in a 'natural' desire replaces a selection that ought to transcend nature, and thus the relationship is improper.

Furthermore, there is a second sense in which the unnatural is understood as a function of the natural: what is wrong, or unnatural, is said to be natural in a person who has been corrupted by education or society. In other words, nature corrupted leads naturally to an unnatural result, a result that is itself "the natural sequel of an unnatural beginning" (*P* 30). In one conversation the faulty education of boys is said to result in "the consequently natural—yet . . . unnatural degree of ignorance and uncouthness of man" (*MP* 339). These examples of the unnatural that naturally results from error suggest that natural in Jane Austen's world refers also to the workings of cause and effect, that is, natural law.

We have seen that civil society is thought to be built on nature and to be proper, in a sense natural, for human beings. This brings us to particular instances in which social relationships and aspects of social life are claimed to be natural and, more important, to the disagreements that such claims can generate. Some characters assume that behavior typical of particular social statuses or strata is natural to the persons occupying those positions. Edward Ferrars, commenting on what he sees as his natural awkwardness, says, "I have frequently thought that I must have been intended by nature to be fond of low company, I am so little at my ease among strangers of gentility!" (*SS* 94). In such cases characters suggest that differences in social status are manifested naturally in behavior. Furthermore, behavior appropriate to the status relationships between interacting characters can also be said to be natural. According to Sir Thomas Bertram, "nothing can be more natural" than the Grants' dinner invitation to Fanny Price: "Mrs. Grant's shewing civility to Miss Price, to Lady Bertram's niece, could never want explanation" (*MP* 218).

Here we again see that what is natural is what is understandable; it wants no explanation because its relevant causes are obvious, even though these causes may emanate from the social order rather than from the nonhuman natural order. In assessing the actions of other people, characters equate what is natural for those others with what, for them—given their temperament and social position—would be "probable, reasonable" (*MP* 305). To explain behavior as natural is to assess the motivations behind it and thereby to construe it in terms of a likely sequence of cause and effect. Thus Edward Ferrars attempts to account for his engagement to Lucy Steele—a relationship that comes to be seen as decidedly unnatural by the end of *Sense and Sensibility*—in terms of his social and emotional situation when he made the engagement at eighteen: "Considering everything, therefore, I hope, foolish as our engagement was . . . it was not at the time an unnatural, or an inexcusable piece of folly" (*SS* 362–63).

It is precisely with respect to these claims for the naturalness of social action that we find the very idea of nature as obvious fact undercut by the texts. By juxtaposing conflicting or contradictory assessments of what is natural, or by presenting in an ironic mode various characters' recourse to naturalness in the rhetoric of explanation, the texts suggest that nature requires interpretation rather than simple empirical observation or discovery. For example, those characters who are shown to be guilty of snobbery sometimes attempt to justify their snobbishness with the argument that the divisions of the social hierarchy are natural. Mr. Darcy claims that his abhorrence of the "inferiority" of Elizabeth's family is "natural and just" (*PP* 192). But in the end, of course, Darcy is proved to have been mistaken, for notwithstanding their difference in rank, Elizabeth is a most suitable marriage partner for him. In other cases people attempt to explain as natural what is obviously the result of human agency. In general, almost any human action, attribute, or failing can be explained as natural, and characters sometimes construe as natural every option in a set of mutually contradictory courses of action. When Elizabeth Bennet assesses the relationship of her sister Jane and Mr. Bingley, she considers the romantic attractions of the former to be "more natural" than "the influence of his friends," who would disrupt the relationship for utilitarian reasons (*PP* 142). At the same time, Elizabeth argues that "nothing . . . could be more natural" than Mr. Wickham's pursuit of Miss King, a pursuit motivated purely by self-interest: "the sudden acquisition of ten thousand pounds was the most remarkable charm of the young lady" (*PP* 149).

In the preceding examples actions motivated by considerations of rank, romance, or self-interest are claimed to be natural, and such claims are called into question by their juxtaposition to other material in the text. However, of all the claims for the naturalness of human actions, those most persistently and seriously undercut— often by a particularly distanced narrative voice—are claims for the naturalness of family solidarity. Family ties are blood ties, and a blood relationship is understood as a fact of nature, a fact that is expected to be manifested both in personal resemblance and in social relationships. But this expectation is more often violated than upheld in the texts. By repeatedly focusing on people related by ties of blood who act 'unnaturally' with respect to one another, the texts fundamentally question the presumed constancy of natural blood ties.

Consider, as a first example, the dispute between Mrs. Jennings and her son-in-law concerning the physical resemblances of an infant: "Mr. Palmer maintained the common, but unfatherly opinion among his sex, of all infants being alike; and though she could plainly perceive at different times, the most striking resemblance between this baby and every one of his relations on both sides, there was no convincing his father of it" (*SS* 248). Though the narration presents Mrs. Jennings's opinion, it does so from a distance, and this dual stance facilitates an examination of her various assumptions of natural resemblance: since the perceived resemblances are mutually contradictory, they must be the product of Mrs. Jennings's interpretation rather than a simple restatement of observable facts of nature. Furthermore, according to Mrs. Jennings, Mr. Palmer is unfatherly—which is to say, unnatural—though she simultaneously recognizes such behavior as common to most men, hence natural to most fathers. In short, Mrs. Jennings's position shows that both natural resemblances and unnatural behavior are culturally constructed.

As a second example consider the discussion of the story of Frank Churchill, estranged in infancy from Highbury circles when his father, Mr. Weston, entrusted him to maternal relations. Frank Churchill is an important presence in Highbury even though he has never been there. Significantly, much of the discussion concerning the geographically distant young man is carried out in terms of what he and his relatives ought naturally to be. At one point several characters try to imagine how his father could have been persuaded to give him up. According to Mrs. John Knightley, "there is something so shocking in a child's being taken away from his parents and natural home! I never can comprehend how Mr. Weston could part with him." But her husband immediately counters by suggesting that "Mr. Weston is rather an easy, cheerful tempered man, than a man of strong feelings." Emma in turn feels compelled to counter Mr. John Knightley, for she "could not like what bordered on a reflection on Mr. Weston" (*E* 96). She declines to speak, however, in the interest of keeping peace, and thus we do not know how she would have constructed her argument. But once again the presumed naturalness or unnaturalness of a mode of conduct is thrown into doubt by the confrontation of various points of view. And we cannot look elsewhere for help in finding the truth, for in the most disinterested narration of the affair we are told only of "some scruples and some reluctance the widower-father *may be supposed* to have felt" (*E* 16, emphasis added). Moreover, this discussion concerning Frank Churchill is a good example of how interpretations that the characters claim to be obvious, because grounded in nature, are shown in the narratives to be motivated by experiences and attitudes not directly related to the material being interpreted. Mrs. John Knightley is depicted as overly motherly, hence her construction of Mr. Weston's behavior as unnatural. Her husband is depicted as overly domestic—indeed, as somewhat misanthropic—hence his defense of Mr. Weston's behavior as not unnatural in a man so unnaturally sociable. Emma tends to quarrel with both Knightley brothers because they refuse to defer to her judgment, hence her willingness to argue the other side of any position advanced by either.

In these and earlier examples the undercutting of presumably natural facts is effected by several devices: the juxtaposition of mutually exclusive points of view, the unfolding of plot to prove an earlier assessment erroneous, or the ironical force of the language itself.

However, with respect to the naturalness of family solidarity, it is often a particularly distanced narrative voicing that undercuts the expectations of the characters. In the final paragraph of *Sense and Sensibility* we are told that Marianne and Elinor, "*though sisters,*" were able to maintain "that constant communication which family affection would naturally dictate" (emphasis added). The first paragraph of *Mansfield Park* describes "an absolute breach" between sisters that is said to be "the natural result" of "a very imprudent marriage." But the most powerful examples of these distanced commentaries concern the relationship of Fanny Price to her natal family. Fanny's relationship with her brother William is described as one instance in which "even the conjugal tie is beneath the fraternal," a rare case in Austen in which the social relationship of siblings conforms to the natural tie on which it is based:

> Children of the same family, the same blood, with the same first associations and habits, have some means of enjoyment in their power, which no subsequent connection can supply; and it must be by a long and unnatural estrangement, by a divorce which no subsequent connection can justify, if such precious remains of the earliest attachments are ever entirely outlived. Too often, alas! it is so.—Fraternal love, sometimes almost every thing, is at others worse than nothing. But with William and Fanny Price, it was still a sentiment in all its prime and freshness, wounded by no opposition of interest, cooled by no separate attachment, and feeling the influence of time and absence only in its increase. (*MP* 235)

Moreover, that the relationship of Fanny and William is a rare case is shown by the casual and, to Fanny, disappointingly cool, relationship that she has with her parents and most of her other siblings. We should remember that this situation results from the unnatural break between sisters—between Fanny's mother, on the one side, and Lady Bertram and Mrs. Norris, on the other—which opened *Mansfield Park,* and that the family will be reconnected only by a similarly unnatural marriage between the siblinglike cousins Fanny and Edmund. The facts of rupture and reunion question the received wisdom concerning what siblings will naturally be to one another: that they will not be romantic partners is challenged by an incestlike marriage, and that they will never be distant is challenged by the matter-of-fact presentation of the three sisters' mutual estrangement: "So long divided, and so differently situated, *the ties of blood were little more than nothing*" (*MP* 428, emphasis added).

CHAPTER THREE

Family, Connections, and Incest

Family ties, "the ties of blood" (*MP* 428), are one of the most important social facts in the world of Jane Austen's texts. Blood relationships are believed to be grounded in the material facts of nature: that family members both resemble and love one another follows ineluctably from the natural fact of their blood ties, and though the texts themselves often undercut this belief, it remains, among the characters at any rate, a relatively unquestioned presupposition. On the other hand, affinal relationships—referred to most often by the term *connection*—are explicitly understood as a product of human choice. Thus the terms *family, blood,* and *relations,* on the one hand, and *connections,* on the other, represent the distinction between the natural and that which is constructed by civil society. And in the domain of family relationships, incest represents the perversion of confounding human choice and natural fact, producing an unnatural and immoral relationship.

Family has two important meanings to the actors in Austen's world. It frequently refers to all the residents and immediate dependents of one household. In this sense it can include not only a married couple with their children but also guests, servants, apprentices, and, perhaps, an adopted cousin or other young person. The heads of a family are often referred to as its master and mistress, titles that relate them particularly to servants, as well as to boarders, apprentices, and young people generally. Thus, in the texts, family extends beyond a modern nuclear family. Because servants are usually behind the scenes in Austen's novels, a late-twentieth-century reader can easily miss this subtle but significant difference. Nevertheless, a number of passages make the extended sense of family clear. In *Mansfield Park* a "whole family assembling regularly for the purpose of prayer" includes "housemaids and footmen" as well as "master and mistress" (86–87). A governess, Miss Taylor, is said to have "been in Mr. Woodhouse's family" for many years (*E* 5), and mention of adopted children as family members is fairly frequent, as the examples of Fanny Price, Frank Churchill, and Jane Fairfax show (*MP* 10; *E* 17 and 164). Finally, we have the case of "a most respectable Girls Boarding School" that is described as one of "two large Families" visiting Sanditon (*MW* 387).

Family has another important use in the texts—as a term for a patriline. The use of family in this sense pertains primarily to the higher ranks of society. For the landed classes, the family is a corporate unit organized around a landed estate passed on, generation after generation, from father to eldest son. This second usage adds a sense of temporal continuity to the sense of spatial contiguity present in family qua household. It is to this second usage that Samuel Johnson's dictionary refers in describing a family as "a course of descent; a genealogy." Such a family theoretically consists of all the lineal descendants, living and dead, of its founder. In practice, there can be variation from the ideal, as when, in the absence of lineal heirs, the line is continued through collaterals. In general, younger sons, particularly if they fail to distinguish themselves, and daughters, if they fail to make a good marriage, are dropped from genealogies in the course of time. The working of such genealogical amnesia is suggested by the narrative's ironic commentary on one family's use of a nickname to refer to an undistinguished, deceased son: "He had, in fact, . . . been nothing better than a thick-headed, unfeeling, unprofitable Dick Musgrove, who had never done any thing to entitle himself to more than the abbreviation of his name, living or dead" (*P* 51).

Though a family estate can be held by females in default of male heirs, the family dies out if the name is not passed on. The family as patriline is symbolized by birth, blood, name, and place. These symbols are embodied in individuals who are endowed with a particular birth and blood, a particular name and place, by virtue of being born into a particular family. As attributes of individuals, they are seen as natural—in the sense of 'given by nature'—and are opposed, in common language, to acquired and selected features.

It is interesting to compare the range of distinctions within the texts to those listed in Johnson's dictionary. Among the definitions that Johnson gives for *blood* are "family; kindred," and "descent; lineage." Under *birth* we find, among others, "extraction; lineage," and "rank which is inherited by descent." Thus both blood and birth are defined in terms of lineage and descent, though blood seems to refer more to actual membership in a group sharing the same blood, while birth refers to the social status that a person enjoys because of his membership in a particular family. This distinction is similar to that in the texts. There blood, as a symbol of family or of a person's membership in a family, is conceived of as shared substance. For example, a man who has scorned and abandoned his family is said to have slighted "the very blood he belonged to" (*P* 9), and children "of the same family" are said to be of "the same blood" (*MP* 235). Birth, on the other hand, designates a person's social status on the basis of his or her family origins. Anne Elliot is said to have "claims of birth, beauty, and mind" (*P* 26), while her father objects to the navy because it is "the means of bringing persons of obscure birth into undue distinction" (*P* 19).

Family names are significant both as symbols of identity and prestige and as social exchange tokens. People drop (as we say) names in conversation, or display the visiting cards of people with prestigious names—in both cases, to express publicly their intimacy with people of rank. Sir Walter and Elizabeth Elliot, for instance, place the cards of a dowager viscountess, a collateral relative of theirs, "wherever they might be most visible" (*P* 149).

A family's name is intimately linked to its place of residence, itself a named estate or house; three of the six novels—*Sense and Sensibility, Mansfield Park,* and *Persuasion*—begin by mentioning the name and place of the central family of the novel. The term *place* also refers to position in the social hierarchy. Social place is intimately linked to physical place, since social status is a function of the ownership of property, and the preeminent form of property is land. There is thus a direct correlation between the magnificence of a family's place—its house or estate—and the importance of its place in society.

In addition to household and lineage, *family* can refer to the children of a husband and wife distinguished as a separate group. The expression "family of children" is used frequently in the texts, and the similar expressions "family of cousins" and "family of young ladies" can also be found. Finally, family is occasionally used in one of our contemporary senses to refer exclusively to a married couple and their children living together privately in a home. However, it is never used in a second contemporary sense to refer to all of one person's relatives.

If we turn once again to Johnson's dictionary, we find, as in the Austen texts, that family refers primarily to a household community or to a community of descent. Beginning with the second edition, of 1755, we find the following entries for *family*:

1. Those who live in the same house; household.
2. Those that descend from one common progenitor; a race; a tribe; a generation.
3. A class; a tribe; a species.

The sixth edition (1785) adds, as the third entry, "a course of descent; a genealogy," with the previous third entry being listed fourth. This more explicit recognition of the family as a community of descent might correspond to what historians have seen as the increase, during the latter part of the eighteenth century, in the use of the rhetoric of genealogy and rank to label newly acquired social positions as traditional and natural (Thompson 1963: 11–14; Spring 1963: 277). The problematics of the creation of supposedly natural relationships will come to the fore shortly in our discussion of the degree to which presuppositions about family can be negotiated.

In opposition to the family, which is understood to be given, or inherent—something received *as is* rather than something created—

connections are explicitly conceived of as man-made, and hence negotiable. The term *connection* is most frequently used in the texts to refer to affines or to specific marriages or proposed marriages. It is also frequently conjoined with its complementary opposite, as in the phrase "family and connections," which recurs as a summary description of the social identity of a character being introduced either by the narration or by one character to another: "Mr. Yates's family and connections were sufficiently known to him, to render his introduction as the 'particular friend,' another of the hundred particular friends of his son, exceedingly unwelcome" (*MP* 183).

The syntactic and lexical opposition of family and connections, then, signifies a cultural opposition between the natural, or given, and the man-made, or constructed. However, despite this apparently clear-cut distinction, connection can also be used to refer to people who might in other contexts be termed blood relations or family—to people as near as a parent (*NA* 205, *E* 145), sibling (*P* 30), grandparent (*MP* 121–22), or first cousin (*P* 74–76). In such cases the use of connection, as opposed to family or relation, stresses the social—hence constructed and mutable—dimension of the kinship tie, as opposed to what the characters see as its natural basis in blood. The social histories of various people represented in the texts suggest that in Austen's world of kinship, one's family relations become one's connections as people move out of their natal households. Whether a particular person is referred to as family or as a connection depends not on the presence or absence of immutable genealogical bonds but on contextual features of the kinship tie in question. These contextual features depend on the life cycle of individuals and the developmental cycle of households, and sometimes on personal preferences as well.

Marriage is the crucial moment in the life cycle when young people leave their natal households to establish their own conjugal households. A young person considering marriage, or being considered by others as a potential marital connection, acquires a social identity newly detached from the parents who have hitherto been the closest of family relations. In the following passage Eleanor Tilney and Catherine Moreland discuss a letter bringing news of a young woman, a Miss Thorpe, who has apparently jilted Catherine's brother in favor of Eleanor's:

> Miss Tilney, at Catherine's invitation, now read the letter likewise; and, having expressed also her concern and surprise, began to inquire into Miss Thorpe's connexions and fortune.
> "Her mother is a very good sort of woman," was Catherine's answer.
> "What was her father?"
> "A lawyer, I believe.—They live at Putney." (*NA* 205)

If we are to understand the nuances of kinship implicit in the terms of this passage, we must remember that before Catherine's visit to the Tilneys, she and Miss Thorpe had together frequented Bath under the tutelage of parents or parental representatives—hence with the kinship status of daughters submissive, rather than merely connected, to parents. Those earlier scenes of the novel make the present passage clear: Miss Thorpe's parents are now discussed as her "connexions" because she is on the point of establishing a new social identity defined in terms of a new and relatively independent household.

In general, the developmental cycle of the household makes connections out of family relations as near as parents, children, and siblings. Consider the case of Mr. Knightley and Emma, whose brother and sister, respectively, are married to one another. This married couple and their children, who reside in London not far from Emma's residence in the county of Surrey, are said to be Emma's and Knightley's "mutual connections." Similarly, from the perspective of the London Knightleys, Emma, her father, and Mr. Knightley are "their Surrey connections" (*E* 9, 91). The passages from which these quoted phrases are drawn show that brothers, sisters, children, and grandchildren can all be termed connections. That the Knightley brothers are now connections to each other, as are the Woodhouse sisters and the elder Woodhouse daughter to her father, suggests the drawing apart of family members into separate households. This process can be intensified when the movement of persons between households is accompanied by personal disputes, irresponsibility, or lack of emotional ties. Thus Mr. Knightley crit-

icizes Frank Churchill, adopted away from his father in early childhood, for never visiting his father: "he may have learnt to be above
his connections, and to care very little for any thing but his own
pleasure. . . . If Frank Churchill had wanted to see his father, he
would have contrived it" (*E* 145).

Connections, then, are the product of human choice and effort,
and as such can become the object of the strategic politics of marriage and courtship. People choose to create, maintain, and destroy
connections. Much of the scheming in the novels is the work of
ambitious parents and siblings who aim to forge advantageous connections, through their children or siblings, for themselves and their
families. Sometimes people work to maintain connections, as when
the normally proud Elliots fawn before some noble cousins: "Family
connexions were always worth preserving" (*P* 149). On the other
hand, if one of two connected families feels that association with the
other is socially harmful, they may frown upon or refuse choices
that would perpetuate the connection. Mary Musgrove exhibits this
attitude toward a projected marriage between the family into which
she married and its matrilateral cousins: "it would be quite a misfortune to have the existing connection between the families renewed"
(*P* 75). A connection between individuals of friendship or business
may be "dissolved" by the parties concerned when mutual good
feeling or utility is no longer present (*PP* 201). Mr. Darcy severs his
relationship with Mr. Wickham in *Pride and Prejudice,* destroying ties
established by their fathers. In *Mansfield Park* Sir Thomas takes his
eldest son with him to the Caribbean in order to "detach" him from
some "bad connections at home" (*MP* 32).

The conception of mutable connections contrasts strongly with
the conception of naturally given and ideally eternal bonds of family.
And, by comparison, it does indeed seem as if the characters more
frequently, and with greater latitude, exercise their control over the
meaning of connections, accepting the perceived naturalness of family as a limitation on their freedom to act. Nonetheless, though the
tie of blood—the familial community of descent—is conceived of as
a natural fact, given and permanent, there are moments when its
naturalness is created and the unalterable fact is altered without perversion. These moments, clearly perceived by the characters as un-

usual, typically stem from transitional situations such as death and marriage, when the characters must negotiate the possibility, if not the necessity, of rearranging the patterns of their natural relationships. For example, the new mistress of Norland Park, Mrs. John Dashwood, easily convinces her husband to ignore the injunction of his dying father, who had asked his son to care for his second wife and his daughters by her. Mrs. Dashwood couches her argument in terms of genealogical distance and the negotiability of all but the closest blood ties:

> And what possible claim could the Miss Dashwoods, who were related to him only by half blood, which she considered as no relationship at all, have on his generosity to so large amount. It was very well known that no affection was ever supposed to exist between the children of any man by different marriages. . . .
>
> ". . . What brother on earth would do half so much for his sisters, even if *really* his sisters! And as it is—only half blood!" (*SS* 8–9)

At the moment of transition, when an estate passes between generations and one household replaces another as the occupants of that estate, Mrs. John Dashwood attempts to rationalize her attack on what had previously been a natural tie.

A more dramatic case involves Edward Ferrars, whose mother disowns him when he refuses to renounce an engagement that she does not approve. None of the characters knows quite how to react to this situation, which reflects how anomalous the characters consider it. Characteristically, we get no definitive version of the story, but a number of varying accounts that the characters tell each other about what they have heard of the matter. In John Dashwood's narration to his half-sisters, Elinor and Marianne, Edward is described as "stubborn" and "unfeeling," and Mrs. Ferrars as the injured party who is justified in her vow never to speak to her son again. Marianne cries out against this view "in an ecstacy of indignation," but John Dashwood mistakes her exclamation for a censure of Edward—which he judges "very natural," though she meant to censure the mother's conduct as unnatural. John Dashwood himself professes to pity Edward because, as he sees it, Edward has foolishly deprived himself of the situation to which he was "born" (*SS* 266–68). Edward's younger brother, Robert Ferrars, agrees with his mother's position, suggesting, if only metaphorically, that the disowned son does not deserve to live: "He must be starved, you know;—that is certain; absolutely starved" (*SS* 300). Later, after Robert has been disowned for a similar crime and Edward grudgingly reinstated by Mrs. Ferrars as her son, a narrator's voice emerges from the narration with ironic distance. As in Robert's comment about starving Edward, the text employs terms of life and health ("annihilation," "resuscitation") that ironically emphasize the naturalness of the relationship between parent and child: "Her family had of late been exceedingly fluctuating. For many years of her life she had had two sons; but the crime and annihilation of Edward a few weeks ago, had robbed her of one; the similar annihilation of Robert had left her for a fortnight without any; and now, by the resuscitation of Edward, she had one again" (*SS* 373).

This passage recalls the final paragraph of *Sense and Sensibility* and the opening paragraph of *Mansfield Park,* where, as we have seen, a particularly distanced narrative voice undercuts any presuppositions that characters (and readers) might entertain with respect to the immutability of the natural ties of blood. In the texts we repeatedly find the characters manipulating situations that they nonetheless believe to be naturally given and immutable. But only in unusual situations do the characters explicitly discuss their construction of the natural, or even realize that such constructions are possible. For these characters, to describe something, such as family, as a natural fact symbolically tames the concept: it persuades the characters that they lack the ability and moral standing to introduce innovative interpretations of their received understanding of such concepts as blood ties and family. On the other hand, because connections are conceived to be man-made, characters more willingly and openly manipulate them, and discuss their own role in doing so.

The preceding discussion enables us to see a fundamental ambiguity in the characters' cultural conceptions. The natural ties of blood, which are conceived of as given and immutable, are created anew by marriage and dissolved by it as well: dissolved because marriage detaches people from their natal families, yet created anew in the community of blood that will exist between the husband, wife, and their offspring. Marriages thus provide for a continual realignment of social relationships, even though the ideology of the patrilineal family presupposes a timeless and natural continuity in blood and affection. Significantly, many characters are aware of the disruptive effects of marriage. For example, for Mr. Woodhouse, "matrimony, as the origin of change, was always disagreeable" (*E* 7). And Anne Elliot is repeatedly "struck" by the lack of concern her married sister shows for her natal family, though her marriage took her only three miles from them (*P* 42). Despite such awareness, people maintain their belief in the ideal of continuity, even validating their pedigree retrospectively with fictive family histories that they soon come to believe themselves (*E* 310). In sum, marriage creates ties expressed in a rhetoric of nature.

The symbolic function of marriage in manufacturing the continuity of familial tradition is at once masked and buttressed by its sacred quality. Marriage is meant to be exclusive and permanent, and this feature distinguishes it from other connections. This distinction is nowhere as clear as in the progress of a successful courtship—of one, that is, that ends in marriage. During courtship the potential alliance is treated as a proper object of meddling and manipulation, but once the marriage is agreed to, and further, once it is made, it is considered all but inviolable. We have already mentioned that an engagement is supposed to preclude all other potential relationships, but, of course, engagements are broken. The conception that engagements establish a marriage is not an inviolable rule of behavior but a guide for interpretation: breaking an engagement is negatively marked. In *Mansfield Park* Sir Thomas is so disappointed when he returns to England and meets his prospective son-in-law, Mr. Rushworth, that he tells his daughter that he will arrange for the engagement to be dissolved despite "the embarrassing evils of a rupture." When Maria responds that she has no intention of "breaking through her engagement," Sir Thomas is relieved: "It was an alliance which he could not have relinquished without pain" (*MP* 200–201). By contrast to his reluctant willingness to act to break off the engagement, Sir Thomas does not indulge Maria's destruction of the marriage after the wedding, and Maria, who had sought to return to her father's household, is supported instead "in an establishment . . . in another country" (*MP* 465).

While people begin and end courtships, and even "break through" engagements, marriage is considered inviolable. The selection of a spouse excludes all other potential spouses, both at the time of the selection and in the future. By contrast, the choice of friends or business associates does not exclude the selection of other such connections. This distinction from other types of connections makes an important meaning of marriage clear: marriage is the only connection that creates a new family—a new natural unit—and, as the only humanly constructed relationship that produces natural ties, it is uniquely modeled as permanent and natural. Marriages should be forever, and because of this, they should be made in harmony with the natures of the two parties, both their personal natures and their families' natural social status. Thus marriage, which creates natural ties anew, is unique among connections in its exclusivity and permanence. Its uniqueness is manifest in the reaction of the characters to adulterous violations of marriage vows, as in Maria Bertram's sad story, as well as in their reaction to a very different boundary: incest.

Incest is the selection of a natural family member as a partner in a marriagelike relationship: it is the confounding of natural ties and connections. Marriage ideally provides a regularized, and perpetual, transition between natural ties of family and humanly constructed connections, for in marriage two people are removed from their natural attachment to their families and united in a selected attachment that will in turn generate new natural ties. Moreover, marriage masks and transcends this transition: the compatibility between the selected partners is, in its own way, considered to be natural, and thus a marriage connection is simultaneously a human creation *and* a part of nature's design. In sum, marriage represents a claim to reproduce the natural order socially and the social order naturally. An incestuous match short-circuits the process: by preempting the social role in reproduction, incest forestalls the transcendent unification of the social and natural orders. Since incest is the selection of what is (already) given, no transition to a (new) natural attachment is realized. Furthermore, to select a person to whom one is already necessarily tied is not to select at all. By denying the complementarity of nature and selection in marriage, incest marks—rather than mediates—the opposition between the two.

Austen's novels respect the taboo on incest linguistically; nonetheless, we shall see that her texts implicitly examine the taboo, even in the word's absence. As we have argued, the novels make the relevant distinctions between romantic partners and siblings quite evident. John Thorpe, to recall one example, distinguishes between his sisters and other young ladies in choosing his partners for rides in his carriage. Catherine Morland, to recall a second case, distinguishes between sisters and romantic partners when she interprets Henry Tilney's entrance with a young lady. And in *Mansfield Park* (250) William Price tells his sister Fanny that they will be able to dance together because no one in the neighborhood will know of their sibling ties.

Of all the novels, incest is closest to the surface in *Mansfield Park*. Early in the novel Sir Thomas Bertram considers inviting a poor niece, Fanny Price, to come and live at Mansfield Park, and in his deliberations Sir Thomas envisions potential problems: "He thought of . . . his two sons—of cousins in love, &c." His sister-in-law, Mrs. Norris, responds that his fears of a poor match for one of his sons are groundless:

> My dear Sir Thomas, I perfectly comprehend you, and do justice to the generosity and delicacy of your notions. . . . You are thinking of your sons—but do not you know that of all things upon earth *that* is the least likely to happen; brought up, as they would be, always together like brothers and sisters? It is morally impossible. I never knew an instance of it. It is, in fact, the only sure way of providing against the connection. Suppose her a pretty girl, and seen by Tom or Edmund for the first time seven years hence, and I dare say there would be mischief. The very idea of her having been suffered to grow up at a distance from us all in poverty and neglect, would be enough to make either of the dear sweet-tempered boys in love with her. But breed her up with them from this time, and suppose her even to

have the beauty of an angel, and she will never be more to either than a sister. (*MP* 6–7)

"Brought up . . . together like brothers and sisters," the union of the cousins would be "morally impossible." Here Mrs. Norris's argument brings out two components of the cultural conception of siblinghood, and the relation of these to the idea of incest. In the fullest sense of the term, siblinghood is a relationship based on both blood and what we might call coresidential childhood. As the narrative in *Mansfield Park* tells us, "children of the same family" (siblings) have "the same blood" and "the same first associations and habits" (*MP* 235). Each of these elements, the biological and the biographical, creates a tie among those who share them. An incestuous choice is one that takes in either of these components of siblinghood. For example, the attachment of Edward Ferrars and Lucy Steele may be considered quasi-incestuous because Edward and Lucy, though not blood relatives, have grown up together. They form their engagement while both are minors residing with Lucy's uncle; and Edward later remarks that he chose Lucy because she was the only woman he had known: "Lucy appeared everything that was amiable and obliging. She was pretty too—at least I thought so *then,* and I had seen so little of other women, that I could make no comparisons, and see no defects" (*SS* 362). Thus the selection of a close childhood acquaintance is fundamentally not a selection, since no comparison is made. By contrast, the incest taboo demands that marriage, and the subsequent natural ties of siblings, be formed on the basis of a real selection.

The discussion between Mrs. Norris and Sir Thomas is extraordinary, for there is no other discussion of incest in the texts. The characters' silence indicates an apparent unanimity concerning the absoluteness of the contrast between romantic partners and siblings. Yet the characters do not exhaust the texts, for the narrations around their silence repeatedly raise the issue of incest. Elizabeth Elliot in *Persuasion* and Emma Woodhouse in *Emma* are said to take the place of their deceased mothers in their fathers' households, and both have unusual problems making marriages of their own. Elizabeth never marries, and Emma insists throughout most of the novel that she will stay unmarried. Moreover, even after her selection and acceptance of Mr. Knightley, she thinks that marrying him "would be incompatible with what she owed to her father, and with *what she felt for him*" (*E* 416, emphasis added). Finally, Emma and Mr. Knightley not only delay their marriage in deference to Mr. Woodhouse's feelings, but after their wedding they avoid breaking up the relationship between father and daughter by taking the extraordinary step of living in Mr. Woodhouse's home, even though Mr. Knightley owns the even more worthy Donwell Abbey estate.

Emma's and Knightley's deviation from the standard residence rule alters the fundamental exclusivity of marriage, for it creates Emma's marital connection without detaching her from her ties to her father, and in the view of at least one neighbor, husband and father "living together" is a "shocking plan" (469). And this, as we shall see in chapters 5 and 6, is the point: some of the most satisfactory conjugal arrangements invert the most basic norms and surprise the most conventional expectations. Reflect again on *Mansfield Park*. The novel opens with a description of incest as "morally impossible," and ends with one of the very marriages precluded by Mrs. Norris's argument: Fanny Price marries her cousin Edmund with whom she was raised. Furthermore, in the eyes of their attentive friends and relatives their long relationship is unremarkably siblinglike. Austen's narration emphasizes the point. When Edmund first thinks of marrying Fanny, he wonders "whether it might not be a possible, an hopeful undertaking to persuade her that her warm and *sisterly* regard for him would be foundation enough for *wedded love*" (*MP* 470, emphasis added). Thus in *Mansfield Park* neither the social rules defining a desirable marriage nor even the most uniformly held social rules defining a possible marriage control human interactions. In *Mansfield Park,* as in all the texts, social behavior is determined neither by natural laws nor by collectively held conceptions, but is constructed and interpreted in terms of malleable cultural concepts.

CHAPTER FOUR

Hierarchies of Choice

Our discussion of incest in chapter 3 suggests that even the most axiomatic social rule is open to negotiation and interpretation. The taboo on incest marks an inner limit to endogamy, but the limit lacks any fixed, natural, or objective location: it can be placed variously in social action. In this chapter we argue similarly that for Austen, there are no precisely defined ranks—in the sense of a social hierarchy composed of bounded groups or classes—that unambiguously place individuals and families relative to one another. Nonetheless, considerations of rank are a pervasive concern in the texts, and inseparable from the endless discussion of marriage. Indeed, disputes about the desirability and value of particular marriages can often be traced to questions of rank, which present ambiguities that cannot be reduced to any one point of view.

A first glance at Jane Austen's world would seem to reveal a clearcut distinction between the low, vulgar, and servile, on the one hand, and the civil, genteel, and elegant, on the other. Yet hierarchy, we argue, is not well understood by studies that seek to delineate, enumerate, and order social strata. As numerous social historians and sociologists have noticed, often with a sense of anxiety, if not embarrassment, the boundaries between social classes are often vague, often contextually variable, and often traversed. Families and individuals rise and fall, and within a community the evaluation of any person's rank or standing is rarely an uncontested fact.

Thus we would be led hopelessly astray were we to depict hierarchy in Austen's world as a social institution composed of discrete, substantive, and unambiguously ranked entities. We shall instead follow Louis Dumont, who has defined hierarchy as the "principle by which the elements of a whole are ranked in relation to the whole" (1970: 66). To avoid misunderstanding we explicitly recognize that the whole is neither a natural object, discrete and bounded, nor knowable as such. To the degree that it takes shape, it is constructed by active interpreters—including both retrospective analysts and contemporary actors—in particular relationships to it. Moreover, precisely because they are not determinative rules for behavior, cultural principles do not generate an integrated sociocultural unit; they are, rather, patterns for interpretation. As we stated at the outset, such principles fundamentally allow their own opposition; that is, they are established only by distinction, and it is the contrasted pair (itself established, at another level, by distinction to some other principle, and so on) that is constituted, and not any individual constituent principle. Thus social hierarchy must not be interpreted in terms of a cultural model but with cultural model*s*: not only do people differ in their evaluations of personal and familial status, but, as we shall argue, they may differ as well in their understanding of the criteria or principles according to which relative worth is assessed.

Hierarchies of Choice

Throughout the Austen novels characters concern themselves with the mutable fortunes of their relative social positions. People quite consciously and publicly evaluate other people with reference to this hierarchical distinction, often expressing their evaluation in terms of social graces and spatial or geometric gradients—"delightful, charming, superior, first circles, spheres, lines, ranks, every thing" (*E* 359).

Our initial concern is to elucidate the principles, or ideals, that structure both the characters' understanding of social status and their
pragmatic attempts to establish, through their communicative interactions, particular hierarchical relations. We begin with the related
concepts of *independence, dependence,* and *choice,* which recur throughout the texts' complex discourse of status.

To be independent is to be governed only by one's own will; in
other words, to have the power as an individual to make choices and
to be governed by those choices alone. By contrast, to be dependent
is to be governed by the will of others—to have others either choose
for one, or to be oneself the choice of others. These two possibilities
are ranked: it is better to be independent than dependent, "better to
chuse than to be chosen" (*E* 17),[1] better to be followed than to
follow (*P* 272)—for it is better to be an individual who can, to borrow Louis Dumont's term, "encompass" others than an incomplete
person who depends on superiors.[2] Indeed, in the Austen texts a
person dependent on another is included within the latter's social
identity and is thus not fully a person in his own right. As C. B.
Macpherson (1962) has argued in his analysis of English political
theory, to be dependent on another is to be incomplete as a human
being. As such, the value attached to independence—the power to
choose and select—is thought to characterize the highest, most civilized form of human existence. Those individuals with the most independence represent the high point of civil society and have the
greatest power to order society hierarchically. Comparisons of social
status are made in terms of the principle of independence. Most
individuals find themselves independent in relation to some—that
is, above them—and dependent on, or beneath, some others. But

1. Note that the cross-cultural record shows us that this value—this principle of
hierarchy—is not a natural desire common to all human societies: among the
Arapesh, "not to choose, but to be chosen, is the temptation that is irresistible"
(Mead [1935] 1963: 140).
2. In his introduction to the English edition of *Homo Hierarchicus*, Louis Dumont
introduces the term *encompass* with a quotation from one of his earlier essays: "a
hierarchical relation is a relation between larger and smaller, or more precisely
between *that which encompasses and that which is encompassed*" (1970: xii).

the categorical superiority of independence over dependence is stated unequivocally by most of the characters, even in cases where the independence is relative. As Mr. Knightley says, "when it comes to the question of dependence or independence . . . it must be better to have only one to please, than two" (*E* 10).

Different degrees of independence are attributed and accorded to different features of social identity: age and generation, sex and marital status, and class. Within the family, children are dependent on parents, wives on husbands. Among families, those with landed property are more independent than those without land. In general, young are dependent on old, and women on men. Let us examine each of these relationships of relative dependence in turn.

1. Offspring are dependent in relation to parents. Children are dependent on their parents' choices and indebted to them for their care and protection. Children are said to look up to their parents and to owe them gratitude and obedience. Parents encompass children, acting and choosing for them. This often causes difficulties in courtship, for dependent children cannot choose their spouses without parental approval. Thus the Dashwoods attribute Edward Ferrars's baffling reluctance to engage himself to Elinor Dashwood, with whom he is apparently in love, to his dependence on his mother's wishes: "His want of spirits, of openness, and of consistency, were most usually attributed to his want of independence, and his better knowledge of Mrs. Ferrars's dispositon and designs. . . . The old, well established grievance of duty against will, parent against child, was the cause of all" (*SS* 101–2).

The day-to-day authority exercised by parents over children is nowhere more evident than in Sir Thomas Bertram's family. According to a neighbor, Sir Thomas "has a fine dignified manner, which suits the head of such a house, and keeps every body in their place" (*MP* 162). When Sir Thomas left for the Caribbean, his daughters "were relieved . . . from all restraint" and "felt themselves immediately at their own disposal" (*MP* 32). Maria, the oldest daughter, pursues a course of behavior that, as she well knows, her father would never have permitted, beginning a flirtation with the charming Henry Crawford after having engaged herself to the wealthy but stupid Mr. Rushworth. When Sir Thomas returns, the frivolities of the young people stop at once; Sir Thomas's daughters complain that their lives have become dull.

For Maria, this renewed submission is intolerable, and she marries Mr. Rushworth, personally inferior as he is, in order to escape from the "restraint which her father imposed" (*MP* 202). Maria's use of marriage to escape from her father suggests why marriage can be a source of conflict between parent and child: marriage marks the accession of young people, hitherto dependents of their natal families, to the head of their own conjugal families. Furthermore, to marry off children is to "dispos[e]" of them (*PP* 375), and to do so means using one of a limited number of opportunities to make a match advantageous to the social status of one's family.

2. Women are dependent on men. Maria Bertram's marriage gives her independence from her father, but only by placing her in a position of dependence on her husband. Nonetheless, this change is generally regarded as an improvement. The relative independence of a wife, as "the mistress of a family" (*SS* 379), is the highest situation that a woman can aspire to, for, with the exception of the rare cases in which they control estates, women have no means other than marriage to establish themselves. By contrast, men control property, which can come to them either through inheritance or through their efforts in a profession or in business. Men are active, women are passive; a man can exert himself, whereas a woman must wait for a man to act for her (*P* 243, 251). Women must wait to be the choice of a man, to be given independence by him (*E* 168). Wives must submit their wills to their husbands (*E* 38). In general, as Anne Elliot remarks, "a strong sense of duty is no bad part of a woman's portion [i.e., dowry]" (*P* 246).

3. Eldest sons have more independence than their younger brothers. Only in unusual cases do younger sons become the principal heirs to an estate. The eldest sons of landed families need not depend on a profession or trade. Knowledge of their prospects of independence often causes eldest sons, such as Tom Bertram, to be careless and extravagant (*MP* 20). Tom's reckless gambling compiles debts, which his father pays off by selling a "family-living"—an ecclesiastical position under Sir Thomas's control—that should have fallen to Edmund, Tom's younger brother (*MP* 23). In this case the eldest brother's absolute independence, considered necessary to prevent the dispersal of the ancestral estate, is maintained at the expense of a younger sibling, who must sacrifice a considerable portion of his relative independence to cover the bad choices of the eldest son. As Sir Thomas tells the delinquent heir: "You have robbed Edmund for ten, twenty, thirty years, perhaps for life, of more than half the income which ought to be his" (*MP* 23). By contrast to the independence of eldest sons, younger sons "must be inured to self-denial and dependence," as Colonel Fitzwilliam puts it (*PP* 183), though, as Elizabeth Bennet points out to him, younger sons of landed families may be considerably better off than the Colonel's complaint suggests. Because they are not born to independence, younger sons must be placed 'out' to make their way in trade or in the genteel professions of the army, navy, law, or church, while daughters are placed 'out' to marry. Significantly, the term 'out' is never applied to eldest sons. This absence suggests that a person who is 'out,' be it a woman in want of a husband or a younger son in search of a living, is a person who lacks a well-defined position 'in' society. An eldest son is always 'in' the family he will eventually head, but women and younger sons do not have a permanent place in their natal households. The distinction between the eldest son and his brothers is encoded in the everyday terms of address: Tom, the eldest son, is called Mr. Bertram, but his younger brother must be specified as Mr. *Edmund* Bertram. And Mary Crawford, who wishes Edmund were the principal heir, says, "There is something in the sound of Mr. *Edmund* Bertram so formal, so pitiful, so younger-brother-like, that I detest it" (*MP* 211).

4. *Landed property affords greater independence than other forms of wealth.* The ideal of independence is epitomized by the gentleman of landed property. Land's materiality and naturalness are taken as signs of its permanence, and, by extension, of the permanence of the patriline associated with land. This permanence—the natural fixity of land—is seen as ensuring a continuous and certain production of wealth.

The family itself is defined as a natural social group whose continuity into the past is substantively manifested in shared blood as well as in the continuous possession of land, an extrasomatic substance shared by family members within and across generations.[3] In theory, landed property is given rather than chosen—it comes down from the past to its possessors, who are born to their possession of it. Thus the owner of land can claim a kind of natural independence denied to his contemporaries, though this implies a dependence, even of the highest nobility, on one's ancestors. Such dependence, of course, involves quite different obligations and opportunities than dependence on living contemporaries.

By contrast to people who inherit landed wealth, those in professions or in trade must depend on or defer to their patrons, clients, and customers; they cannot command their own time because they are continually engaged. Thus the profession of law can be likened to "slavery" (*E* 116), whereas only the gentleman without any profession at all can be "disengaged from every tie of business" (*NA* 176). Here we should emphasize that the superiority of the gentleman's situation is a function not of wealth but of the source or independence of his wealth. Though wealth and independence are clearly connected, we must not confuse the two: Willoughby, for example, is said to be "independent," but "there was no reason to believe him rich" (*SS* 71). Professional men and merchants might very well be richer than private gentlemen, yet, continually engaged as they are, they are lower in the hierarchy of independence. Thus there is a general expectation that Admiral Croft will defer to Sir Walter Elliot, even though he is wealthy enough to rent Sir Walter's landed estate when the baronet can no longer afford to maintain it (*P* 17–22, 32).[4]

3. Schneider (1968) has argued that in contemporary America natural ties are symbolized by reference to shared bodily substance, notably blood (i.e., 'ties of blood'). In tracing the conception of natural ties through Western history, we would expand Schneider's analysis of the symbolic value of bodily substances to include other material substances of 'nature.'

4. It is well to insist that the cultural valuation of land is not a function of its objective economic value, though both contemporary and later commentators appeal primarily to the economic aspect in attempting to explain, or to rationalize, its (cultural) primacy. According to J. R. M. Butler, opponents of the Reform Bill of 1832 thought "that property in land had especial claims to rule the State"; "a moneyed man might invest his capital abroad," but "the landed class

The understanding of land as a familial attribute that is given rather than created suggests that the hierarchy of choice is rationalized as natural or given. That children are inferior to parents, younger to older, women to men, and landless to landed is thought to follow inevitably from the respective abilities and natures of each type of person. Many of the characters in Austen's novels routinely assume that talent and conduct depend on birth; that is, on inherited social position. Lady Catherine de Bourgh, for example, asserts that she and her daughter have a superior "natural taste" for music, though neither knows how to play. She even insists that *had* her daughter learned, she would necessarily have been a better performer than the more lowly ranked Elizabeth Bennet, who *does* play (*PP* 173, 176). Similarly, Mrs. Norris assumes that her nieces, the Bertram sisters, are more intelligent than their more lowly ranked cousin, Fanny Price: "There is a vast deal of difference in memories, as well as in every thing else, and therefore you must make allowance for your cousin, and pity her deficiency" (*MP* 19). In both cases the texts ironically examine the presumptions of natural superiority based on social status. What, after all, could be more laden with irony than the ingenuous assertion that a woman who does not play *would* play better than one who already does?

Up to this point we have examined the opposed concepts of dependence and independence as ideals, but if we turn to a consideration of practice, we must recognize a fundamental irony, if not

---

. . . were tied to the country for good or ill. . . . Thus their stake in the nation was greater than all other." This was true even though "from the beginning of the century commerce and manufacturing began to challenge the predominance of agriculture" ([1914] 1963: 246). And modern historians of English landed society repeat the rationalizations of the landed interest they study. G. E. Mingay, for example, discusses the value of land in the eighteenth century in largely cultural terms—land was more highly esteemed than other forms of property that may well have been more "profitable"—but goes on to justify this cultural valuation by invoking the familiar native rationalizations: "Above all, land was immovable and indestructible; and the very permanence of land gave stability to the society that was based upon it" (1963: 3; cf. Thompson 1963: 4).

tension, within this opposed pair: to attain independence is not to isolate oneself from others (that is, to be truly independent and separate) but to create particular relationships in which one's choices dominate or override those of others. Independence, then, is a relationship between two or more, and not—contrary to the professed cultural model—a property or essence within a person, or even a patriline.

Not only does independence involve a degree of dependence explicitly denied by the very term *independence,* but dependence on superiors can be used to gain advantage over others, particularly others of comparable social status. Because a dependent person is contained within a patron's social identity, relative subordinates can gain status vis-à-vis their near equals by accepting the patronage of status superiors. The highly placed Sir Walter Elliot and his daughter Elizabeth, for instance, are servile to their cousins the Dalrymples—members of the nobility—in order to flaunt this association to others: "they had the cards of Dowager Viscountess Dalrymple, and the Hon. Miss Carteret, to be arranged wherever they might be most visible" (*P* 149).[5]

Moreover, those who are independent may be said to depend on their dependents in at least two senses. First, the landowning gentry are dependent on their rural laborers, despite the fiction that landed wealth is independent. Second, those in the "first circles" (*E* 359) are

5. Such readiness to become dependent, even where there is no economic need to do so, should be contrasted to the situation of those who struggle to maintain independence in the face of economic misfortune. For example, when Mrs. Dashwood and her three daughters are left homeless after the death of Mr. Dashwood, they become the dependents of Sir John Middleton, "a gentleman of consequence and property" who is portrayed both as good-hearted and as desirous of having dependents. By contrast, "the independence of Mrs. Dashwood's spirit" leads her to decline many of the amenities that Sir John offers, even though the Dashwoods must sharply curtail their participation in genteel society as a result (*SS* 23, 40). Taken together, the examples of the Dashwoods and the Elliots show that the value of independence cannot be reduced to economic terms. For the calculation of relative rank on the basis of conspicuous consumption, and for Austen's careful depiction of such calculations, see Copeland (1986).

often forced into matrimony with inferiors in order to provide themselves with the financial means to maintain their station and the human means to reproduce it. Because their superiority is marked by their abstention from productive activities—they must be "disengaged from every tie of business" (*NA* 176)—and because their status is commonly expressed and performed by conspicuous consumption, genteel families often ruin themselves by spending more than their income. Their continued independence must thus be reestablished, often through exchanges in which they obtain financial resources from those of lower rank but greater wealth, just as Sir Walter Elliot rented his family estate to a newly wealthy naval officer. More generally, new wealth can be incorporated into ancestral status through marriage. Such exchanges, most particularly marriage, occur as an always present bootstrap in the social system; that is, they occur as the condition of possibility where inferiority (of one type or dimension) can be transformed into superiority (of another). In brief, dependence can be transcended to produce and renew independence. Such social mobility, we argue, must be understood as an internal, dialectical feature of the hierarchical system.[6]

In more general terms, though the performance and creation of status relations presupposes previously accepted status relations (themselves variously understood), it is important to note that the hierarchical relationships *between* actors are never established once and for all. Rather, they must be enacted and reenacted without any assurance that the prior social relations will be reproduced. Social relations are not fixed without the possibility of alternatives. People may, from time to time, agree about the terms of their relationship, thereby allowing alternatives to remain undeveloped, but this is only a limited case. At least potentially, relationships can always be negotiated, negated, and transformed; the messages meant to establish

6. This suggests that the rise of the bourgeoisie was an immanent feature of the aristocratic order. Similarly, our analysis suggests that individualism (culturally defined in terms of power to exercise independent choice) was not a new element introduced by an emergent middle class but was an element of aristocratic life adopted, and thereby changed, by the wider social order (cf. Macfarlane 1978; Morrill 1979: 69–74; O'Boyle 1979; Spring 1983: 65–67; Corrigan and Sayer 1985: 84–86, 130–31).

particular hierarchical relationships can be accepted or contested—in either case self-consciously or not. Thus both the reenactment of prior hierarchical relations (so-called continuity) and the construction of new hierarchical relations (so-called change) alike emerge from the common process of the symbolic construction of social relations. Moreover, even when there is no manifest social change, cultural rules implicitly and inherently establish the possibility of contrasting alternatives, any of which can potentially serve as the basis for a manifestly different social formation.

Pragmatic Symbolics: The Social Construction of Status Relations

As we examine the particular interactions in which people seek to establish various hierarchical relations vis-à-vis others, it is important to note that we cannot make lists of distinctively upper-class or distinctively lower-class activities. Rather, the mutability of hierarchy occurs, at the level of social practice, because of the ambiguity of social communication and exchange: an invitation can be issued from a superior to an inferior as a command, or it can be issued from the latter to the former as an offering of homage. In both cases the invitation can be either accepted or rejected, and just as acceptance generally indexes an acceptance of the hierarchical terms of the relationship, so rejection indicates the contrary. In both cases the message and its response—and the relations both seek to establish—can only be understood in terms of the presupposed hierarchical relations between the parties involved. Moreover, the metacommunicative possibilities of these indexical attentions permit even more complex meanings.

Consider, for instance, the subtleties of hierarchy in Highbury, the setting of *Emma*. The Knightleys' Donwell Abbey estate makes up the largest part of Highbury, which is described as a "large and populous village almost amounting to a town" (*E* 7). The Woodhouses' Hartfield, though the village's second-largest estate, is described as "a sort of notch in the Donwell Abbey Estate." Nonetheless, in Emma Woodhouse's view, "their fortune, from other sources, was such as to make them scarcely secondary to Donwell Abbey itself, in every other kind of consequence" (*E* 136). Indeed, throughout most of the novel Emma acts as if the Woodhouses and Knightleys were coequal as the village's preeminent families. In addition to these two high-status families, Highbury contains at least six other families with claims to being a part of the local elite of genteel society: the Westons of the Randalls estate ("a little estate adjoining Highbury" [*E* 16]) and the Eltons, Bateses, Coles, Coxes, and Mrs. Goddard. Two other families—the Martins and the Perrys—are neither completely outside this group nor entirely within it. Other families in Highbury cannot be counted as members of genteel society—for example, the prosperous Fords, who run "the shop first in size and fashion" in Highbury (*E* 178).

Though it is clear that families are ranked in terms of the concepts of relative gentility and vulgarity, we cannot specify any exact relationship between these families, since such relationships are at once manifested and rearranged by their social interactions, particularly through the medium of visits and invitations. Emma, for instance, frequently invites people to Hartfield because her father, though fond of society, rarely ventures from his estate. However, those invited are not thought of or treated alike. "The chosen and the best" include the Westons, Mr. Knightley, and Mr. Elton, and a "second set" includes Mrs. and Miss Bates and Mrs. Goddard. Significantly, Emma conceives of this distinction in terms of "sets," that is, in terms of categorical separation and distinction. Emma invites the second set, who are described as "ladies almost always at the service of an invitation from Hartfield," only when the first set is not available (*E* 20, cf. 208–9). Furthermore, in most cases Emma's perception of the social order is accepted and enacted by others. For example, when any of Emma's first families call on the Bateses without invitation, their visits are understood as charitable attentions: the asymmetry of such visits is often marked by gifts, such as foodstuffs, chosen to ease the Bateses' tight financial situation. The guest lists at parties at the Westons' (*E* 117–19) and at Donwell Abbey (*E* 355–57) show that other members of the first set share Emma's perception of the composition of Highbury's elite, though not necessarily her perception of the hierarchy within this elite or their relationship to social inferiors.

If we shift our attention to the second set, additional segments of Highbury society come into view, and we see that the social hierarchy involves overlapping social relationships rather than impermeable boundaries. Though Emma neither invites nor receives invitations from the Perrys or the Coles, both families regularly exchange visits and drink tea with the Bateses (*E* 17–18). Moreover, not only are the Perrys indirectly connected to the best families through their social relations with members of the second set, but the frequent visits of Mr. Perry, the local apothecary, to Mr. Woodhouse are described as "one of the comforts of [his] life" (*E* 19), though these visits occur in the form of a professional service.

The situation of the Martins is like that of the Perrys in its complexity. Robert Martin is described by Mr. Knightley as "a respectable, intelligent gentleman-farmer" (*E* 62). Although Robert Martin is Mr. Knightley's tenant, the former dines at the house of Mr. Knightley's brother, John, an attorney in London (*E* 472), and furthermore, Robert Martin dines with the Coxes. Neither dinner, however, results from a formal invitation to the Martins as a family; both are sequels to business meetings with Mr. Martin and involve him alone. Still, the willingness of the Coxes and the John Knightleys to share their table with him shows that Robert Martin is not considered to be beyond the scope of genteel society.

Emma recognizes that the relationships between members of her second set and such families as the Perrys and Coles indirectly connect her to people she considers vulgar. Indeed, Emma dislikes visiting the Bateses because such visits put her "in danger of falling in with the second rate and third rate of Highbury" (*E* 155). Contrary to Emma's pretensions, then, social interactions cut across her first and second sets. As such, the social hierarchy of genteel Highbury can be conceived not only as separate "sets," "circles," or "spheres" (*E* 359) but as an interlocking chain in which all families, even if they can be ranked, are linked. From our ethnographic perspective we do best to accept both these models and to observe the complex interactions in which each model is used to enact hierarchical relations.

Some of the novel's most interesting examples of such interactions involve the Coles, precisely because this family actively tries to elevate itself in Highbury's social hierarchy. Through their success in trade the Coles have become increasingly wealthy, and they try to convert their newly won property into peer relations with Highbury's genteel society. Through additions to their house and changes in their social life they attempt to introduce themselves into the higher levels of the Highbury hierarchy; that is, into a domain discussed in terms of a rhetoric of ancestral origins:

> The Coles had been settled some years in Highbury, and were very good sort of people . . . but, on the other hand, they were of low origin, in trade, and only moderately genteel. . . . The last year or two had brought them a considerable increase of means. . . . With their wealth, their views increased; their want of a larger house, their inclination for more company. They added to their house, to their number of servants, to their expenses of every sort; and by this time were, in fortune and style of living, second only to the family at Hartfield.[7] Their love of society, and their new dining-room, prepared every body for their keeping dinner-company. (*E* 207)

The change in the Coles' social habits leads Emma to suspect that they will invite even her to attend one of their parties, and she decides that "nothing should tempt *her* to go, if they did," for "they ought to be taught that it was not for them to arrange the terms on which the superior families would visit them." The Coles do indeed plan a dinner party with the best families of Highbury, but Emma, perhaps by design, receives her invitation after Mr. Knightley and

7. Here Emma's narration places Hartfield at the pinnacle of the social hierarchy, notwithstanding Donwell Abbey's admitted superiority in size. This discrepancy suggests that the reader might question whether characters in Highbury other than Emma would accept her account of her preeminent position in the social hierarchy. Indeed, we suggest that the narrative voice of *Emma* subtly undercuts its explicit presentation of Highbury through Emma's eyes. This would substantially alter the standard reading of the novel, converting the story into a tale of hypergamy that occurs, ironically, in spite of the heroine's initial overconcern with social status and rank. For a similar reading see Marilyn Butler (1975: 272–73), who writes that "Emma's conception of herself as first lady is a kind of figment of the mind."

the Westons have received—and accepted—theirs. Before Emma
has received her invitation, Mrs. Weston tries to assure Emma that
the absence of an invitation shows that the Coles "will not take the
liberty with you," but Emma knows that Mr. Knightley, whom she
admits as her equal, has been invited, and she feels slighted: "She
felt that she should like to have had the power of refusal; and afterwards, as the idea of the party to be assembled there, consisting
precisely of those whose society was dearest to her, occurred again
and again, she did not know that she might not have been tempted
to accept" (*E* 208). When the Woodhouses' invitation arrives (along
with a flattering explanation for its delay) very shortly before the
day of the party, its previous absence and the acceptance of the
invitations by others proves sufficient to increase its worth in
Emma's mind, and she is persuaded to accept: "She owned that,
considering every thing, she was not absolutely without inclination
for the party" (*E* 208). In brief, Emma cannot on her own stop the
Coles, since they have already succeeded with the other members of
her first set.

The Coles' party is an intricately structured event that reflects the
multiple sets of Highbury society. The dinner itself, in addition to
the Coles, Emma Woodhouse, Mr. Knightley, and the Westons, includes "one other family, a proper unobjectionable country family,
whom the Coles had the advantage of naming among their acquaintance, and the male part of Mr. Cox's family." The postdinner evening party includes an even larger group, for to the diners are added
the female Coxes (described as "less worthy" than the males), Miss
Bates, Miss Fairfax (the Bateses' niece), and Miss Smith (Emma's
protégée) (*E* 214). Significantly, the Coles, who until this time have
been portrayed as part of the Bateses' set, now are able to raise
themselves above the Bateses by relegating them to a second set of
after-dinner guests.

Emma's vision of a static community in which she can control the
assignment of social status is belied by the Coles' dinner-party. She
can control neither the choices and initiatives of others nor the reactions of still others to those choices and initiatives. Emma may consider the Coles vulgar, and their invitation pretentious, but she
cannot impose on others of her first set to follow her. Similarly,

Emma's fears of contact with such people as the Bateses and the Martins are not shared by Mr. Knightley, the Westons, and the Eltons. Mr. Knightley sees Emma's reluctance to visit the Bateses as a "deficiency" in social responsibility (*E* 155), but Emma, by contrast, sees Mr. Elton's willingness to dine with the Coles as one of his most disturbing "failings," indicating, in Emma's view, a lack of rigor in marking his social superiority (*E* 213).

In general terms, Jane Austen's representation of Emma's world suggests various competing views or models of the Highbury social hierarchy, none of which is granted absolute authority. Emma, always looking down from the peak of the system, interprets the social hierarchy as a series of distinct steps or levels—that is, to extend the architectural image, as a staircase. By contrast, the upwardly mobile Coles deal with the social hierarchy as a continuous, ramplike spiral. Mr. Knightley, Mr. Elton, and other characters develop still other images of and attitudes toward Highbury's social order. We suggest that no single character's actions and attitudes can tell us what the social order *really* was, and thus that multiple perspectives be kept in mind when trying to understand social hierarchy as narrated in Austen's novels.

Relations of Alternatives

Different perceptions of social status can be explored not only in terms of architectural images but in terms of moral sensibility. Characters disagree both about how individuals ought to behave within the social hierarchy and about the very basis of rank; that is, which attributes of individuals ought to determine their moral and social worth. In terms of differing judgments about proper behavior, it is useful to distinguish three philosophies and styles of exchange as ideal types. At one extreme are the *selfish exchangers*—characters who fetishize independence in their attempt to keep material and social resources, and ultimately themselves, to themselves. At the other extreme are the *sociable exchangers*—those whose zeal for keeping company outweighs their concern for differences of rank. For both selfish and sociable exchangers, the practice of exchange is largely insensitive to the interests and feelings of their exchange partners. By contrast, there are those who conceptualize hierarchy in terms of differing responsibilities: for them, social superiority entails duties toward inferiors, and every rank, from the highest to the lowest, is understood to have inalienable rights as well as responsibilities attached to it.

The *responsible exchanger* is well illustrated by Mr. Knightley of Highbury. According to Emma, "you might not see one in a hundred, with *gentleman* so plainly written as in Mr. Knightley" (*E* 33). In this instance Emma is referring to appearance and manners, but, as she gradually learns, the essence of Mr. Knightley's gentility lies not in outer forms but in the constancy with which he fulfills his social responsibilities. Mr. Knightley, the largest landowner in Highbury, attends to his less fortunate neighbors promptly and unfailingly. Moreover, he offers aid with tact and discretion, motivated by the "wish of giving pleasure" rather than the expectation of "conferring obligation" (*E* 378).

Many other characters belong to families that are said to be the "principal inhabitants" (*PP* 12) of their villages. Thus when Marianne Dashwood marries Colonel Brandon she becomes not only "mistress of a family" but "patroness of a village" (*SS* 379), and when Admiral Croft rents Kellynch Hall, he takes over the social responsibilities of its owner and former occupant (*P* 125). These responsibilities oblige the owner of an estate "to be liberal and generous,—to give his money freely, to display hospitality, to assist his tenants, and relieve the poor" (*PP* 81).

The ability to exercise patronage, offer charity, and generally aid others—in brief, to encompass them as dependents—is a key mark of social superiority. Even when unable to afford the common accoutrements of gentility, distressed gentlefolk sometimes attempt to maintain a minimal dignity by aiding those who are even poorer than themselves. For example, Mrs. Smith of *Persuasion*, an invalid who is "unable even to afford herself the comfort of a servant," still exerts herself in order to find "the means of doing a little good to one or two very poor families" (*P* 153–55). Once her most elementary needs have been satisfied, Mrs. Smith's conception of herself and of what her social place has been requires that she turn her attention to the aid of her inferiors—precisely because the initiation of charitable transactions reconfirms her (vulnerable) status as a gentlewoman.

Yet more than openhandedness, more even than genteel manners, is required of those who exchange responsibly. The key lies in what Mr. Knightley calls "English delicacy towards the feelings of other people" (*E* 149). To behave "dishonourably" is to behave "unfeelingly" (*MP* 225), whereas responsible exchangers would see their charitable actions as being characterized by "genuine attention to other people" (*SS* 338). English delicacy combined with responsible attention means more than making sure that one's dependents are provided for. Patronage, attention, and charity are to be offered tactfully and inconspicuously, with proper account taken of the rank and situation of the dependent. Overwhelming attention and charity are oppressive, even "insulting" (*E* 288), requiring gratitude that cannot be outlived. Thus the good breeding of gentlefolk is manifested not only as the difference in manners between genteel and low but also as the proper degree of consideration shown toward members of all social ranks.

By contrast to the responsible exchanger, the selfish exchanger is primarily interested in amassing wealth. For example, to John and Fanny Dashwood the idea of independence means freedom from the claims of dependents. For them, any obligation to inferiors—such as the payment of annuities to former servants—"takes away one's independence" (*SS* 11). As we saw in chapter 3, Fanny even convinces John to ignore his father's last request to assist his widow and daughters. Fanny argues successfully that the daughters (John's half-sisters) have no claim on his generosity (*SS* 8–9). Similarly, Sir Walter Elliot and his daughter Elizabeth, when forced to "retrench," cannot bear to "sacrifice . . . journeys, London, servants, horses, table." However, Elizabeth easily persuades her father "to cut off some unnecessary charities" (*P* 9–13). Thus both the Dashwoods and the Elliots privilege a narrowly private use of familial resources over wider social responsibilities.

At the other extreme, sociable exchangers are inclined to bring people together without regard to their relative rank and character. Frank Churchill, to Emma's dismay, is so fond of dancing that he is perfectly willing to bring together families that Emma would keep apart: "He could not be persuaded that so many good-looking houses as he saw around him could not furnish numbers enough for such a meeting [a ball]; and even when particulars were given and families described, he was still unwilling to admit that the inconvenience of such a mixture would be any thing, or that there would be the smallest difficulty in every body's returning into their proper place the next morning" (*E* 198).

Associated with this sort of indiscriminate social mixing is a lack of tact in the offering of services. Mr. Knightley finds such tactlessness in Churchill's gift of a pianoforte to Jane Fairfax. Because of her secret engagement to Churchill, Jane cannot explain his gift to her Highbury neighbors and must therefore suffer as the object of their intrusive curiosity. In Knightley's opinion, the gift "was the act of . . . one too young to consider whether the inconvenience of it might not very much exceed the pleasure" (*E* 446). Sir John Middleton shows a similar lack of sensitivity by pressing his offers of aid to the Dashwoods, his distressed cousins, "to a point of perseverance beyond civility" (*SS* 30).

As philosophies or styles of exchange, the extremes of selfishness and sociability might be characterized in terms of exclusiveness and inclusiveness. The selfish extreme is exclusive: hospitality, visits, and invitations are strictly monitored to yield social interaction only with people of equal, or, if possible, higher rank than the initiator. By contrast, the sociable extreme is inclusive: visits, invitations, and general hospitality are not aimed at dividing people according to social place. Rather, the sociable person seems determined to gather round himself, in his house and at his table, the maximum number of friends. The vaguest connections, based on kinship, locality, or rank, can be pressed into the service of this goal.

The sociable, selfish, and responsible exchangers represent different views of how people ought to act with respect to hierarchical distinctions. Austen's novels also depict substantial disagreements about the very basis of those distinctions. These disagreements are expressed both by differences between characters and by the relationship of the narrative voice to the social action being narrated. We have already examined some examples in which the narrative challenges conventional beliefs in the naturalness of social hierarchy. Lady Catherine de Bourgh may believe her daughter to be naturally superior in musical ability to Elizabeth Bennet, but the narrative exposes the ludicrousness of her belief. Moreover, Lady Catherine's insistence on Elizabeth's low connections and their inevitable personal inferiority is contrasted, with a profound and sustained irony, to Lady Catherine's own personal inferiority—her rudeness and mediocre abilities. In general, Austen's novels show us a world in which desirable personal attributes are randomly distributed throughout the social hierarchy. There are as many villains and fools among the highest ranks as there are on the fringes of genteel society, just as virtue and good sense are as likely to be found in the Robert Martins and Elizabeth Bennets as in the Emmas and Lady Catherines.

There is also explicit recognition and discussion of this issue on the part of some of the characters. *Persuasion,* for example, focuses on the different understandings that characters entertain concerning the relationship of rank and personal worth. Characters such as Sir Walter Elliot and Lady Russell assume that personal merit is a function of ancestral rank. Sir Walter, who cares only for rank and personal appearance, is presented—indeed, ridiculed—as hopelessly vain and foolish (*P* 4). Less easily dismissed is Lady Russell, "a benevolent, charitable, good woman . . . rational and consistent," who nonetheless "had prejudices on the side of ancestry" and "a value for rank and consequence, which blinded her a little to the faults of those who possessed them" (*P* 11). By contrast, Anne Elliot believes that personal merit confers rather than follows rank.

These opposing points of view inform the novel's ongoing comparison of the landed gentry and the naval profession. This issue first arises as Sir Walter, "distressed for money" (*P* 9), considers renting his ancestral estate. When his lawyer suggests that "this peace will be turning all our rich Navy Officers ashore" and that such officers "make desirable tenants," Sir Walter objects that the naval profession is "the means of bringing persons of obscure birth into undue distinction, and raising men to honours which their fathers and grandfathers never dreamt of." By contrast, Anne reflects on the worthiness of men of the navy: "The navy, I think, who have done so much for us, have at least an equal claim with any other set of men, for all the comforts and all the privileges which any home can give. Sailors work hard enough for their comforts, we must all allow" (*P* 17–19). Some weeks later, when Admiral Croft and his wife take residence at the Elliot estate, Anne is unable to lament the change: "she could not but in conscience feel that they were gone who deserved not to stay, and that Kellynch-Hall had passed into better hands than its owners'" (*P* 125).

Later, when Sir Walter demeans himself to reestablish a connection with his noble cousins, Anne objects that Lady Dalrymple and her daughter, without "superiority of manner, accomplishment, or understanding" (*P* 150), are unworthy of pursuit. Throughout the novel we are shown that the rules of conventional wisdom that predict merit on the basis of rank are as likely to be wrong as right, and that interpretive discernment is necessary to assess moral worth and personal abilities. Lady Russell is indeed frequently blinded by her prejudices, while Anne's understanding of rank and human abilities proves to be more attuned to the complexities of social experience.

CHAPTER FIVE

Courting Exchanges and Alter-Cultural Marriages

Within the quotidian civilities of attentions, compliments, and invitations, we find not only the ongoing establishment of hierarchical relations but, closely related to it, the construction of new conjugal bonds. As young, unmarried adults meet people of the opposite sex, they must both select among the set of possible spouses available to them and communicate their interest (or disinterest) to each other. Austen's novels offer readers at least three important perspectives on this complex social process.

First, throughout the novels characters discuss courtship both in terms of general principles of etiquette and propriety and in terms of the specifics of particular cases. From these discussions we can extract a commonly understood set of terms with which people make judgments about the suitability of a particular person as a spouse—for themselves and for others. In addition, these discussions allow us to construct an idealized model of courtship. This normative model is not, of course, what generally happens, nor is it a model that all the characters find compelling; however, it is uniformly recognized as a public standard for presenting oneself to others as someone eligible for marriage and for expressing attraction, encouragement, and refusal. Moreover, it attaches opprobrium to the failure to employ this communicative code.

Second, against the presentation of the general etiquette of courtship the novels set the stories of numerous courting characters. By examining these stories as a set, we can see how various characters in diverse situations employ the ideals of marriage to make choices between potential marital partners and how they communicate their choices through the etiquette of courting civilities. We find that the characters who accept without question the ideals of marriage and the conventions of courtship fail to communicate richly with the person who becomes their partner for life.

Third, as a subset of all the stories of courtship, the heroines' stories play a special role in Austen's oeuvre. Though the heroines and their partners make marriages outside the recognizable boundaries of courtship, they do not, in any simple sense, reject the conventional civilities of courtship, nor the conventional standards for appealing to and discriminating between potential partners. These characters know full well what a particular action conventionally means, but instead of using this code facilely, they creatively comment upon it, pursuing courtships and making marriages that are not so much antisocial as they are alter-cultural. The heroines and their partners follow unusual paths in establishing their marriages (hence the interest of their tales), but their unusual courtships lead to rich communication (hence the promise of their marriages).

In this chapter we will examine the overall process of courtship by comparing these three perspectives, and in the next chapter we will use a similar approach to examine one element of courtship—dance—in greater detail.

Courting Exchanges

Marriage, Mary Crawford tells us, "is a manoeuvring business"—"of all transactions, the one in which people expect most from others, and are least honest themselves" (*MP* 46). Marriage, in Henry Tilney's view, is, like a country-dance, "a contract of mutual agreeableness"—"an engagement between man and woman, formed for the advantage of each" (*NA* 76–77). Despite the sharp contrast in these views, they nonetheless share an important feature of similarity: Mary Crawford sees self-interest where Henry sees reciprocal benefit, but both see marriage as an exchange in which each side gives and receives.

In employing the term *exchange* to describe the transactions of marriage, we purposefully introduce a term from anthropological theory to invite comparisons between the complex marital system of Austen's texts and so-called elementary structures of kinship (Lévi-Strauss, [1949] 1969). Clearly, the marriages in Austen's narrations do not form a classic structuralist exchange system. Though there is a sense in which families exchange sons and daughters to establish alliances, there are no rules that would generate recurring cycles of exchange over generations. Parents and grandparents are frequently active in arranging marriages for their children and grandchildren, but in general their concern is focused on the propriety of a particular match rather than any ongoing exchange between family units. Families do not exchange marriageable children (and their substitutes) with other families; rather, marriageable children are exchanged (by themselves and their families) so that "they belong exclusively to each other" (*NA* 77). In this social system the force of societal values focuses attention on the relationship established between individuals rather than the relationship established between families or larger social units, hence the emphasis throughout Austen's texts on the opinions of the potential husband and wife, expressed, for men, primarily in terms of choice, and for women primarily in terms of acceptance.[1]

1. Lévi-Strauss argues that the passage to complex systems (that is, systems in which marriage is increasingly a matter of individual selection, socially specified only by general prohibitions) involves an indefinite expansion of the sphere and periodicity of cycles of reciprocity. Our comparison emphasizes the resulting focus on the process of individual selection. In particular, the normative principle of inclusion and interrelation through a prescription to exchange (dances, compliments, partners) *generally* is incorporated into the selection process of each individual actor. What is elsewhere a feature of relations amongst social units over many generations is compressed into the civilities of courtship—

The process of selecting a spouse causes the courting characters to interpret each other as signs—items that can be treated as substitutes for each other in terms of a feature of similarity (eligibility) and which must be discriminated in terms of features of difference (various traits of person and situation). At one level, characters of the same sex are interchangeable as potential spouses vis-à-vis characters of the opposite sex, and, at another level, each character must use additional criteria to choose among potential spouses. The criteria employed to discriminate between possible spouses fall into two groups: public and utilitarian, on the one hand, and personal and romantic, on the other. Ideally, these criteria should produce a single interpretation of a character's suitability as a spouse, but, as we shall see, practice is not ideal in Austen's world. Divergences between signs of a character's wealth and rank and signs of the same character's personal traits often make selecting a marriage partner problematic.

To complicate matters further, the process of selecting a spouse involves not just making a decision but being another's choice as well: the selection must be reciprocal. In courtship each person must select among possible spouses while presenting him- or herself in as favorable a light as possible. In addition, each person must be able to exchange messages expressing interest or refusal with many possible spouses. The mutual exchange of two people in matrimony does not result from an isolable act of individual decision making but from an interactive process of selection and communication. The process of making a marriage does not begin with an explicit decla-

---

even, as we shall see in chapter 6, a single evening of dancing. Thus the indefinite expansion of the periodicity of exchange cycles also involves a compression of time to the dimensions of individual decision making (cf. Lévi-Strauss [1949] 1969, particularly pp. 474–77).

The anthropological historian Alan Macfarlane has presented extensive data on English marital exchanges between the thirteenth and nineteenth centuries; for material particularly relevant to the present chapter see Macfarlane (1986: 119–73). For a critique of Macfarlane and further discussion of English kinship see Strathern (1989).

ration of interest or love to a particular person but with the general message of interest in, and availability for, matrimony.

Both men and women declare their general interest in matrimony by engaging widely in social exchanges with potential spouses. They exchange attentions and admire each other. Men invite women to dance and compliment their accomplishments, and women accept these favors with gratitude. Propriety prescribes an evenhanded treatment of all potential spouses, so preferential behavior stands out as a clear sign of particularity. In the exchange of these attentions, interest is expressed through a degree of exclusivity, and refusal through neglect. Henry Crawford, who simultaneously leads on Julia and Maria Bertram, demarcates the norm of evenhanded civility with his own transgression: "Each sister believed herself the favourite . . . his manners being to each so animate and agreeable, as to lose no ground with either, and just stopping short of the consistence, the steadiness, the solicitude, and the warmth which might excite general notice" (*MP* 115).

In the interactions of potential spouses, men and women alike are admired for the same attractions. These include, first, those personal features of mind, manner, and appearance that can create and justify romance, as the following passages from *Persuasion* and *Pride and Prejudice* illustrate:

> He was . . . a remarkably fine young man, with a great deal of intelligence, spirit and brilliancy; and Anne an extremely pretty girl, with gentleness, modesty, taste, and feeling. (*P* 26)
> "To Jane herself" [i.e., independent of the quality of her family connections], she exclaimed, "there could be no possibility of objection. All loveliness and goodness as she is! Her understanding excellent, her mind improved, and her manners captivating." (*PP* 186)

Taken together, these descriptions show that both men and women are admired for possessing intelligence and good looks. Nor should we conclude that spirit is a predominantly masculine, and gentleness a predominantly feminine, trait. Emma holds up Mr. Elton to her protégée, Harriet Smith, as a model of gentleness (*E* 34), Elinor Dashwood praises Edward Ferrars for his modesty and taste (*SS* 19–

21), and Elizabeth Bennet's spirit and liveliness of mind (*PP* 380) are important attractions to Mr. Darcy.[2]

In addition to such personal attractions, the familial attributes of wealth, rank, and connections can appeal to utilitarian aspirations. Once again, these qualities are equally desirable in men and women: Sir Thomas Bertram commends Mr. Crawford to Fanny Price on the basis of his "situation in life, fortune, and character" as well as his personal charm (*MP* 316), and Emma denigrates Mr. Elton's choice of Miss Hawkins on similar grounds: "*What* she was, must be uncertain; but *who* she was, might be found out; and setting aside the £10,000 it did not appear that she was at all Harriet's superior. She brought no name, no blood, no alliance" (*E* 183). In sum, both men and women should possess the romantic attractions of beauty, intelligence, and manners, and the utilitarian attributes of birth and wealth. Those persons who possess all of these are presumed (at least unreflectingly) to be the most admired and the most marriageable.

Though both men and women may admire and be admired, and though both would wish to possess the same personal and familial attractions, their roles in exchanging attentions are not symmetrical. As Henry Tilney expresses it, in courtship (as in dance) "man has the advantage of choice, woman only the power of refusal" (*NA* 77). It is the man's prerogative to ask for a woman's hand, in marriage or the dance, and this rule places women in a relatively passive position. Nonetheless, in spite of this asymmetry, courtship involves reciprocal relations between a gentleman and a lady, as the narrator's account of the youthful romance of Frederick Wentworth and Anne Elliot stresses: "It would be difficult to say which had seen highest perfection in the other, or which had been the happiest; she, in receiving his declarations and proposals, or he in having them accepted" (*P* 26). Indeed, women who accept a proposal are said to have made their "choice" or to have "chosen" their "lot" (*PP* 125, 216, 377; *E* 64).

Furthermore, a woman's power of refusal is not insignificant, for

2. As K. C. Phillips has pointed out, such words as *pretty, beauty, bloom,* and *glow* can be applied to men as well as to women (1970: 80).

it is almost always respected. When Elizabeth Bennet refuses her foolish cousin's offer of marriage, her father supports her decision despite her mother's appeal to him to "make Lizzy marry Mr. Collins" (*PP* 111). Though Collins initially interprets Elizabeth's refusal as an instance of "the established custom of your sex to reject a man on the first application, . . . as [is] consistent with the true delicacy of the female character" (*PP* 108), there is little evidence to support Collins's account of female conventions. Elizabeth assures him that there are few "young ladies . . . who are so daring as to risk their happiness on the chance of being asked a second time" (*PP* 107), and the novels contain no cases in which women pursue such a strategy. Furthermore, as the difficult courtships of both Elizabeth Bennet and Anne Elliot show, men do not easily repeat proposals once refused. In sum, though Collins justifies his refusal of Elizabeth's refusal in terms of established custom, the narrative points not to social convention but to his self-deceiving vanity. Ultimately, Elizabeth's refusal has the power to send the annoying Mr. Collins away.

Similarly, in the more authoritarian family of Mansfield Park, timid Fanny Price's refusal of Henry Crawford is respected, though the stern head of the household, Sir Thomas Bertram, is at first so angry at Fanny's decision that he reduces her to tears with the following condemnation:

> I had thought you peculiarly free from wilfulness of temper, self-conceit, and every tendency to that independence of spirit, which prevails so much in modern days, even in young women, and which in young women is offensive and disgusting beyond all common offence. But you have now shewn me that you can be wilful and perverse, that you can and will decide for yourself, without any consideration or deference for those who have surely some right to guide you. (*MP* 318)

Later, however, Sir Thomas tells Fanny that "you cannot suppose me capable of trying to persuade you to marry against your inclinations" (*MP* 330), and he acts accordingly toward her, though he continues to believe that the proposed match is highly desirable.[3] And finally, women can always act to elicit a proposal—they can play the passive role actively, a matter we shall consider below.

Though men more actively express initial preferences, women are more active in presenting themselves as attractive partners, for they publicly present their accomplishments. Like manners, accomplishments are acquired attributes that can balance the gifts of nature, or, in unlucky cases, stand in their stead: "she was eagerly succeeded at the instrument by her sister Mary, who having, in consequence of being the only plain one in the family, worked hard for knowledge and accomplishments, was always impatient for display" (*PP* 25). Female accomplishments include skill in various domestic arts and "a thorough knowledge of music, singing, drawing, dancing, and the modern languages" (*PP* 39). Gatherings of unmarried adults include both discussions and presentations of these accomplishments: "Elinor had painted a very pretty pair of screens for her sister-in-law, which being now just mounted and brought home, ornamented her present drawing room; and these screens, catching the eye of John Dashwood on his following the other gentlemen into the room, were officiously handed by him to Colonel Brandon for his admiration" (*SS* 234). Similarly, eligible ladies are regularly asked to present musical performances (*SS* 35; *PP* 24, 100; *E* 229). Moreover, these concerts do not include married women: "Here ceased the concert part of the evening, for Miss Woodhouse and Miss Fairfax were the only young-lady-performers" (*E* 229). A short time later Mrs. Weston sits down to play the piano, but only to provide music to accompany dancing. Once married, women do not present their accomplishments, and many lose these skills of courtship:

> The instrument was unlocked, every body prepared to be charmed, and Marianne, who sang very well, at their request went through the chief of the songs which Lady Middleton had brought into the family on her marriage, and which perhaps

---

3. Only in Colonel Brandon's pathetic story are we told of a young woman who is forced to marry against her will (*SS* 205–6).

had lain ever since in the same position on the pianoforté, for her ladyship had celebrated that event by giving up music, although by her mother's account she had played extremely well, and by her own was very fond of it. (*SS* 35; cf. *E* 277)

Gratitude, one of the most important of civil exchange tokens, is yet another element that provides evidence of the prescribed complementarity, rather than equivalence, in men's and women's roles in courtship. As an exchange token, gratitude can only be a response; it is at once an acknowledgment of attentions received and a preliminary return that holds the promise of increasing returns in the future. Gratitude is the appropriate response for the reception of all types of services and favors, from the affection and care bestowed on children by parents to the exercise of political patronage for dependents and retainers. In all cases "a grateful heart" is one that "could never receive kindness without wishing to return it," even though the return cannot be made in the same currency (*MP* 26). In romantic matters gratitude is the natural return for admiration, attentions, and affection; even when these cannot be returned in kind, they must be acknowledged with gratitude. Like admiration, gratitude can be either a masculine or a feminine sentiment, but, in contrast to admiration, it is more frequently a feminine response to male initiative. Since it is men who have the advantage of choice, it is women who must be grateful to men for taking the initiative at the key moments of courtship.

Against the general background of civil exchanges, initial preferences—the beginnings of affection—are thought to be natural and spontaneous. For instance, when Elizabeth asks Darcy when and how he began to love her, he is able only to reply, "I was in the middle before I knew that I *had* begun" (*PP* 380). According to the characters' shared ideals, the spontaneous feeling of attraction cannot truly be based on a utilitarian feature but only on those marked as personal. Wealth makes someone a desirable marriage partner in general, but as a love affair, marriage is supposed to contain an element of personal compatibility: hence the romantic appeal of individuated traits of persons.

Nonetheless, romantic attraction is not enough; it must be developed by a public courtship that allows spontaneous, natural feelings to be fixed. As Charlotte Lucas (who establishes a narrowly utilitarian marriage in the absence of spontaneous attraction) explains, attraction must be reinforced if it is to lead to marriage:

> it is sometimes a disadvantage to be so very guarded. If a woman conceals her affection with the same skill from the object of it, she may lose the opportunity of fixing him; and it will then be but poor consolation to believe the world equally in the dark. There is so much of gratitude or vanity in almost every attachment, that it is not safe to leave any to itself. We can all *begin* freely—a slight preference is natural enough; but there are very few of us who have heart enough to be really in love without encouragement. In nine cases out of ten, a woman had better shew *more* affection than she feels. Bingley likes your sister undoubtedly; but he may never do more than like her, if she does not help him on. (*PP* 21–22)

Similarly, Mrs. Gardner (Elizabeth Bennet's aunt) emphasizes that passionate feelings do not, on their own, signify very much: "'It seems likely to have been a desirable match for Jane,' said she. 'I am sorry it went off. But these things happen so often! A young man, such as you describe Mr. Bingley, so easily falls in love with a pretty girl for a few weeks, and when accident separates them, so easily forgets her, that these sort of inconstancies are very frequent.'"

Moreover, when Elizabeth protests that Mr. Bingley was "violently in love," Mrs. Gardner replies: "But that expression of 'violently in love' is so hackneyed, so doubtful, so indefinite, that it gives me very little idea. It is as often applied to feelings which arise from an half-hour's acquaintance, as to a real, strong attachment. Pray, how *violent was* Mr. Bingley's love?" (*PP* 140–41).

Jane's disappointment, in this case, results precisely because the convention of fixing spontaneous and natural reciprocal attraction through a public courtship allows interested observers to disrupt romantic affairs that do not also meet utilitarian standards. As Jane's sister Elizabeth argues, the sisters and friend of Mr. Bingley convince him to give up his attachment because in their eyes a connection to the Bennet family is beneath him:

> "You persist, then, in supposing his sisters influence him."
> "Yes, in conjunction with his friend."
> "I cannot believe it. Why should they try to influence him? They can only wish his happiness, and if he is attached to me, no other woman can secure it."
> "Your first position is false. They may wish many things besides his happiness; they may wish his increase of wealth and consequence; they may wish him to marry a girl who has all the importance of money, great connections, and pride." (*PP* 136–37)

Bingley's advisers actively conspire to keep him from courting Jane: "pointing out . . . the certain evils" of the match (*PP* 198), they discourage him from returning from London to the country neighborhood where she resides; and later they keep him from knowing of Jane's extended stay with her relatives in London (*PP* 371). Similar motives lead Edward Ferrars's mother to employ more brutal methods: she disinherits him when he persists in refusing "a most eligible connection" that she chose for him, while maintaining an engagement that she does not approve (*SS* 266).

To summarize the argument to this point, the conventionally ideal courtship begins with spontaneous attraction, but a permanent state of affairs—an attachment of matrimony—is created by a subsequent series of increasingly exclusive exchanges of admiration, gratitude, and encouragement. Without the exchange of these messages, the uncertain, natural state of liking can never become a permanent, man-made state—can never become an attachment based on fixed commitments. If the beginnings of love are to be transformed into something more, the exchanges must escalate in frequency and value, and they must be increasingly restricted to two people. As exchange with other partners is ruled out, it is said that the affections of the exchangers have become an attachment, and with open and mutual acknowledgment between two parties, an attachment becomes an engagement. If this, in turn, is honored by their families, the state of matrimony is assured.

As young people leave their families and enter the society of adults, they leave behind the given attachments of childhood and enter into newly constructed relationships. To allow this to occur, social conventions first establish widespread, evenhanded social intercourse. This constructs the context of selection and choice, focusing the power and force of social values on individuals and the propriety of the marriages they make. Moreover, the unrestricted exchange of courting civilities creates a background that easily allows the communication of particularity. As Austen's narrations ironically inform us, particularity is easily signified because it interrupts general civility. As Elizabeth Bennet says, "is not general incivility the very essence of love?" (*PP* 141). If love begins spontaneously, without people's conscious notice, it does not proceed with such stealth; rather, developed publicly, love disturbs civility and establishes both the social possibilities of fixing spontaneous feelings and of foreclosing them. Love may be "uncivil," but it is also "elevating" (*PP* 150), since it takes natural feelings and creates stable ties for reproducing the social order—naturally and properly.

Some Conventional Variations

Though the characters commonly recognize the communicative code of courtship, there is nonetheless a great deal of variation in their courting practices. Much of this variation can be understood by examining two contradictions, or tensions, within the commonly understood principles of courtship. First, there is an inescapable contradiction between the idea that falling in love is natural and spontaneous and the conception of courtship as a series of deliberate exchanges that must conform to established rules of propriety. This leads to the question of "design" in love (*PP* 4): Can people fall in love intentionally, and ought they to do so? Second, there is the problem of evaluating possible spouses in terms of two types of criteria—romantic and utilitarian—that are not always harmonious. These two major tensions are related, for romance is conceived of as a natural, spontaneous process, whereas utility is thought to be attainable through deliberate negotiation and exchange. It would seem, then, that a 'good' marriage must reconcile irreconcilable elements. And this is effectively the position of the texts, which at every turn question not only the concept of a good marriage but the very limits of the category *marriageable* and the processes whereby actors claim to know them. If we are to understand this, we must return to our assertion that courtship is exchange and communication with *others*, and similarly, that the major difficulties of courtship hinge on the problem of how to understand other people.

In examining the communicative potential of various courtship strategies, it is useful to formulate two ideal types: the *romantic exchanger* and the *utilitarian exchanger*. Each type seeks in exchange something other than communication—something other, that is, than an exchange of information, ideas, and experiences that will lead both exchanging parties to a better understanding of the other and themselves. The romantic exchanger cares ultimately for the process of exchange itself, the utilitarian for the goods that can be obtained in exchange; the one is in love with love, the other with wealth and rank. Neither seeks to understand the subjective reality of the exchange partner: for the romantic exchanger, the partners are themselves objects, while for the utilitarian, they are of interest only as possessors of objects.

In their attempted exchanges neither the romantic nor the utilitarian goes beyond self to discover an other. Both aim for objects whose value they have predefined solely in their own terms, without reference to the others with whom they will exchange. These exchange strategies lead to an 'unnatural' result; that is, to marriages with no fundamental personal attachment between husband and wife. Such imbalanced marriages may be compared to incomplete circuits of exchange in so-called elementary systems, for just as a failure to return a gift causes a break in the ongoing cycle of exchange, the privileging of one feature of a good marriage over another deletes a strand from within the complex ties that ideally make every marriage an enduring attachment of mutual love and esteem.

The romantic exchanger believes that marriages should be based on true love, and that true love involves "falling a sacrifice to an irresistible passion" (*SS* 378). True love, in this view, cannot be constructed and cannot result from utilitarian concerns. This ideology is epitomized by Marianne Dashwood and her mother. Mrs. Dashwood makes a virtue of paying no attention, in courting matters, to utilitarian considerations: "It was contrary to every doctrine of her's that difference of fortune should keep any couple asunder who were attracted by resemblance of disposition." Differences of fortune might work in her (and her daughters') favor, or against it, but Mrs. Dashwood is alike unmoved by "motives of interest" and "motives of prudence" (*SS* 15). Moreover, she understands romance very much as love at first sight (cf. *SS* 336), and she judges people immoderately, expressing intense feelings after little acquaintance. For example, her daughter Elinor's observation that Edward Ferrars differs from his sister Fanny is sufficient to commit Mrs. Dashwood wholeheartedly to him:

> "It is enough," said she; "to say that he is unlike Fanny is enough. It implies every thing amiable. I love him already."
>
> "I think you will like him," said Elinor, "when you know more of him."
>
> "Like him!" replied her mother with a smile. "I can feel no sentiment of approbation inferior to love."
>
> "You may esteem him."
>
> "I have never yet known what it was to separate esteem and love." (*SS* 16)

Marianne Dashwood is even more committed than her mother to outward features of manner and appearance, and to those, in particular, that indicate a romantic sensibility. Thus her a priori image of what a lover ought to be serves to guide her judgment of the men that she meets, such as her sister's lover and her own. This image is primarily constructed of external qualities, though Marianne assumes that outer features are a true guide to character—believing, for example, that spirited, fiery eyes "at once announce virtue and intelligence" (*SS* 17). Again like her mother, she despises any regard less than love, as we see in the following discussion with her sister about Edward Ferrars. Elinor begins:

> "I do not attempt to deny," said she, "that I think very highly of him—that I greatly esteem, that I like him."
>
> Marianne here burst forth with indignation—

"Esteem him! Like him! Cold-hearted Elinor! Oh! worse than cold-hearted! Ashamed of being otherwise. Use those words again and I will leave the room this moment." (*SS* 21)

Marianne, then, prejudges both the qualities and emotions of others, even though she would claim that her romantic sensibility is grounded in spontaneity of judgment and feeling. Moreover, such a method may well hinder understanding of those judged by it, for Marianne can be acquainted only with those whom she has created in her own imagination. It is precisely on these grounds that her sister criticizes her opinion of Colonel Brandon, for, as Elinor tells her, the Colonel that Marianne sees has been decided "on the strength of your own imagination" (*SS* 51). Furthermore, Marianne wishes to find nothing but her own opinions in her conversations with a lover: "I could not be happy with a man whose taste did not in every point coincide with my own" (*SS* 17). She finds such a man in Willoughby, whose easy agreement in matters of taste she mistakes for profound identity of character:

> Their taste was strikingly alike. The same books, the same passages were idolized by each—or if any difference appeared, any objection arose, it lasted no longer than till the force of her arguments and the brightness of her eyes could be displayed. He acquiesced in all her decisions, caught all her enthusiasm; and long before his visit concluded, they conversed with the familiarity of a long-established acquaintance. (*SS* 47)

This easily established familiarity, based as it is on the facile performance of agreement rather than the difficult communication of differences (and similarities) of opinion, ends in rupture—Willoughby jilts Marianne for an heiress—and in much unhappiness for both parties.

In contrast to romantic exchangers, the utilitarian exchanger cares only to calculate the advantages of wealth and rank that any potential match affords. We have already seen that Charlotte Lucas would advise women to feign romantic exchanges in order to "fix" men: "Jane should . . . make the most of every half hour in which she can command his attention. When she is secure of him, there will be leisure for falling in love as much as she chuses" (*PP* 22). And Charlotte defends her choice of Mr. Collins by explicitly and purposefully renouncing romance in favor of utility: "I am not romantic you know. I never was. I ask only a comfortable home" (*PP* 125). Examples of this willingness to sacrifice romantic love for utilitarian gain recur throughout Austen's novels where young men seek heiresses and young women are urged or expected to accept the first eligible offer they receive. Fanny Price, for example, is almost overwhelmed by the uniform disapproval provoked by her refusal of Henry Crawford's offer. Her uncle, Sir Thomas Bertram, though he will not impose his views upon Fanny, reacts with horror when Fanny refuses to accept Crawford solely (as far as Sir Thomas knows) because she does not love him. And when Fanny turns to Lady Bertram for comfort, she is told only "that it is every young woman's duty to accept such a very unexceptionable offer as this" (*MP* 333). Fanny's refusal of Henry Crawford is based not only on a heart that is "pre-engaged" (*MP* 326) but on an understanding of Crawford's flawed character that none of her advisers have achieved. The utilitarian exchanger is often as ignorant of the complexities of others as is the romantic, for neither uses courtship to communicate about the problematics of establishing a household and family with someone different from oneself. In some cases utilitarian exchangers cynically accept this lack of communication as inevitable, claiming, in Charlotte Lucas's words, that "happiness in marriage is entirely a matter of chance" (*PP* 23).

Mary Crawford expresses a similar view, though with a brighter wit than Charlotte. Like Lady Bertram, Mary believes that when it comes to marriage, "it is every body's duty to do as well for themselves as they can" (*MP* 289). However, she also has some sense of the dangers of such an attitude, for she characterizes marriage as a "manoeuvering business" marked by deception and disappointment: "I know so many who have married in the full expectation and confidence of some one particular advantage in the connection, or accomplishment or good quality in the person, who have found themselves entirely deceived, and been obliged to put up with exactly the reverse!" (*MP* 46). Despite such knowledge, Mary refuses to abandon her utilitarian strategy. When she finds herself attracted, in spite of herself, to Edmund Bertram, the younger son of Sir Thomas, rather than to Edmund's older brother, "she [is] heartily sorry for it" (*MP*

114), but avoids reexamining her own values and motives on the basis of the new experience. In the end Mary Crawford renounces Edmund, having gained neither self-knowledge nor any understanding of the moral significance of his principles and character.

We have presented the romantic and utilitarian exchangers as ideal types, but, as is to be expected, the characters in the texts are distributed along a continuum between the two. Mary Crawford herself is tempted by romance, though her utilitarian motives prove stronger, and other characters combine romance and utility in differing proportions. It would seem, however, that few do so successfully, for most of the marriages presented in the texts lack mutual understanding and support. Most characters, notably the heroines' parents, select a spouse after a brief acquaintance, taking signs of romantic appeal and social status as a sufficient basis for marriage. Ironically, their fluent performance of conventional courtship rituals is not necessarily functional, for it does not guarantee the formation of stable marriages based on rich communication. Moreover, Austen's narrations show that courtship conventions can be used to misrepresent as well as to convey intentions. Mary Crawford acknowledges this in the passage quoted above, where she describes her many friends who have been "deceived" in courtship (*MP* 46). And Mary's brother, Henry, is a master practitioner of such deceptions. As we saw, he is able to raise the expectations of both Bertram sisters simultaneously while "just stopping short" of any publicly enacted attentions sufficient to give either sister a claim on him (*MP* 115). Thus, as we have argued from the outset, cultural conventions, such as the elaborately patterned civilities of courtship, ensure neither social stability nor social communication. Both clichéd, impoverished communications and misrepresentations are inseparable aspects of the fiction of culture, as are the creative possibilities raised by the heroines' alter-cultural marriages, to which we now turn.

Alter-Cultural Marriages

In contrast to conventional courtships, and even to conventional variations on them, Austen offers the unusual courtship experiences of the heroines, whose marriages, when finally secured, fail to conform to the common understanding of a desirable match. Furthermore, these marriages do not offer any easy, formulaic solution to the problem of finding a suitable partner—neither romance nor utility is embraced, but neither is entirely rejected. In comparing the heroines' marriages to the larger set of marriages within the texts, we find a series of aberrations that both illuminate and question most of the presuppositions about marriage generally held among the characters.

What features distinguish the heroines' marriages from those of other characters? To begin with, the man and woman in these cases know each other unusually well before their engagement, precisely because they do not immediately fall in love and do not get to know each other through the too facilely understood conventions of courtship. The potentially successful relationships of the heroines and their men do not begin with the recognition of natural affinity and passion, nor even with obvious signs of either. For instance, in *Pride and Prejudice* Elizabeth Bennet and Fitzwilliam Darcy begin their acquaintance with a strong dislike for each other, and Elizabeth overhears Darcy commenting unfavorably on her looks. In *Persuasion* Anne Elliot hears a report of a similar comment from Captain Wentworth soon after they meet following an eight-year separation. Anne takes his observation that she was "altered beyond his knowledge" (*P* 60) as painful confirmation of the demise both of her youth and of their earlier romance. In both cases perception proves not to be a given, and each man learns to enjoy his future wife's appearance.

Moreover, both Anne Elliot and Elizabeth Bennet come to understand their future husbands from evidence that lies decidedly outside the domain of courtship. Anne observes Wentworth's capacity to preserve domestic peace broken by an unruly child (*P* 80). Similarly, Elizabeth's understanding of Darcy is altered by knowledge of his domestic relations. Visiting Darcy's estate as a tourist, she hears one of his servants, a Mrs. Reynolds, tell of his fairness and compassion: "This was praise, of all others most extraordinary, most opposite to [Elizabeth's] ideas. . . . Elizabeth almost stared at her.—'Can this be Mr. Darcy!' thought she." After Elizabeth has "listened, wondered, [and] doubted," she concludes that the "commendation bestowed on [Darcy] by Mrs. Reynolds is of no trifling nature. What praise is more valuable than the praise of an intelligent servant?" (*PP* 248–50). Elizabeth's judgment of "the praise of an intelligent servant" should be compared to more conventional estimations of servants' reliability as sources of information. Typically, servants are deployed as mere conduits—that is, as messengers—or are deemed irresponsible gossips: "It was the very event to engage those who talk most, the young and the low; and all the youth and servants in the place were soon in the happiness of frightful news" (*E* 336). By contrast, Elizabeth's trust in a servant's judgment concerning the most serious social and ethical qualities of a master's character is an alter-cultural appreciation of the potential wisdom of social others.

In these extended courtships, then, each woman gets to know her future spouse more as a family member than as a lover. This suggests the even more unusual—almost incestuous—romances of Fanny Price and Emma Woodhouse. Both Fanny and Emma marry men they have known since childhood on an intimate and familial basis. Fanny marries her cousin Edmund Bertram, in whose family she has been raised. As we saw in chapter 3, before the Bertrams adopted her, Edmund's father, Sir Thomas, had expressed apprehension concerning the possibility of romance between Fanny and one of his sons. But his fears had been assuaged by the officious Mrs. Norris, who argued that it would be "morally impossible" for children brought up "together like brothers and sisters" to become lovers (*MP* 6). Throughout the novel Mrs. Norris's advice appears sound. In a social community that takes brief gestures of particularity as signs of a possible marriage (that "jumps from admiration to love, from love to matrimony in a moment" [*PP* 27]), and in a household wary of any signs of particularity between Fanny and her cousins, there are no courting signs between Fanny and either Edmund or his elder brother, Tom. For example, when Edmund dances with Fanny at an important ball, he is thankful to be free of the courting obligation of general civility: "'I am worn out with civility,' said he. 'I have been talking incessantly all night, and with nothing to say. But with *you*, Fanny, there may be peace'" (*MP* 278). That Edmund explicitly denies the necessity for such exchange with

Fanny—and contrasts this to his duties to other dancers (among whom is Mary Crawford, the woman he is, with difficulty, courting)—shows that he takes for granted their preestablished and familial relationship. Moreover, the narration tells us that the "sober tranquillity" of their dancing "might satisfy any looker-on, that Sir Thomas had been bringing up no wife for his younger son" (*MP* 279, cf. 316–17).

Yet Fanny has loved Edmund, in a passively jealous way, almost from the beginning of the novel, though it is difficult to say whether her love is that of a sister or a potential wife. On the one hand, her feelings for Edmund are assimilated in the narrative to her feelings for her brother William: "she loved him better than any body in the world except William; her heart was divided between the two" (*MP* 22). On the other hand, she is protected from the attempted seduction of Henry Crawford because, we are told, her affections are "engaged elsewhere" (*MP* 231). As for Edmund, he acts throughout as Fanny's teacher and adviser (*MP* 22, 113, 152), roles proper for either a spouse or a sibling. We are repeatedly told that Edmund's feelings for Fanny are brotherly (*MP* 374, 444, 460). More surprising still, when he at last decides to marry her, he is willing to court her on the basis of her sisterly affection for him: "it began to strike him . . . whether it might not be a possible, an hopeful undertaking to persuade her that her warm and sisterly regard for him would be foundation enough for wedded love" (*MP* 470).

Edmund and Fanny's relationship, as Edmund notes during their dance, does indeed contrast with the civilities of courtship. Moreover, as the narration points out (without, however, endorsing the view as its own), most onlookers would interpret that contrast conventionally. But the meaning of the contrast is not fixed and determined, and Fanny and Edmund develop romantic intimacy from coresidential childhood alter-culturally.[4]

---

4. The marriage of Fanny and Edmund has been particularly troubling to many twentieth-century critics. G. B. Stern, speaking of Fanny, complains that "Edmund was too like herself" (1944: 64). For Marvin Mudrick, "their final union seems almost narcissistic" (1952: 179). Attempting to show "why the endogamous marriage of Fanny and Edmund is justified," A. M. Duckworth speaks

A similar conversion of familial to romantic affections occurs in the case of Emma Woodhouse and Mr. Knightley. At the beginning of *Emma* Mr. Knightly is described as an "old and intimate friend" of Emma and her father (*E* 9). He often advises the valetudinarian Mr. Woodhouse concerning the management of his affairs and has watched over the precocious Emma as she grew to adulthood. Mr. Knightly is also a brother by marriage to Emma, his younger brother having married her elder sister, Isabella. As in-laws, Mr. Knightly and Emma have the same nephews and nieces, and as we saw in chapter 2, Emma perceives that their ideas about these children are alike (*E* 98). As brother-in-law to Emma, Knightley says, "I have a very sincere interest in Emma. Isabella does not seem more my sister" (*E* 40). As friend and brother, Mr. Knightley plays the role of a dispassionate and sometimes critical adviser to Emma. He is the only person who tells Emma of her faults (*E* 11), and he admits openly to his solicitude for her. After saying that Isabella does not seem more his sister than Emma, he continues without interruption: "[Isabella] has never excited a greater interest; perhaps hardly so great. There is an anxiety, a curiosity in what one feels for Emma. I wonder what will become of her!" (*E* 40).

---

of the impossibility of a "positive marriage" (1971: 37). Darrel Mansell tells us that "Edmund and Fanny are so much alike at the beginning that they almost coalesce." He adds that "Edmund began as Fanny's foster brother, and at the end he still seems closer to that than to a husband" (1973: 137, 142). Finally, R. F. Brissenden has explicitly raised the issue of incest: "The alliance between Edmund and Fanny has distinctly incestuous overtones; and it is these, I believe, that give the relationship . . . its underlying power. . . . Fanny, of course, becomes much more than a sister to Edmund. But her marriage to her cousin, like Tom Jones' affair with the woman assumed to be his mother, invokes the taboo of incest without in fact breaking it" (1975: 165–66). The notion of breaking rules suggests the sociology of deterministic norms against which we have pitted Austen's texts. From our perspective, Austen's narration of a marriage between Fanny and Edmund suggests not broken rules but a displacement, or reinterpretation, of the characters' understanding of the too incestuous closeness of a marriage between siblings. On this notion of 'displacement' of meaning, see chapter 8 below.

Rereading or remembering the novel, one might discern more than fraternal anxiety here and, in general, considerable romantic ambivalence between Emma and Mr. Knightley. To consider a detail of the text that might appear trivial, Mr. Knightley's interest in Emma's intellectual development leads him to "preserve . . . [for] some time" a list of books that she compiled at the age of fourteen (*E* 37). By comparison, the narration subsequently focuses great attention on the romantic significance of Harriet Smith's hoarding of "a small piece of court plaister" and "the end of an old pencil" that had been touched by Mr. Elton (*E* 338–39). To consider a more obvious example, the normally even-tempered Mr. Knightley takes an almost irrational dislike to Frank Churchill, the eligible bachelor whom public opinion deems a likely match for Emma: "On his side, there had been a long-standing jealousy, old as the arrival, or even the expectation, of Frank Churchill.—He had been in love with Emma, and jealous of Frank Churchill, from about the same period, one sentiment having probably enlightened him as to the other" (*E* 432).

For her part, Emma insists in an equally irrational fashion that "Mr. Knightley must not marry" (*E* 224), though only some two hundred pages later does she come to understand that her complete sentiment is "Mr. Knightley must marry *no one but herself*" (*E* 408; emphasis added). However, even this seemingly definite expression of her feelings is no more than an assertion that she wants no one else to marry Mr. Knightley; it is not an avowed desire to marry him herself, and a mere seven pages later we learn that Emma has not entirely given up her often repeated claim that she will never marry: "Could she be secure . . . of his never marrying at all, she believed she should be perfectly satisfied.—Let him but continue the same Mr. Knightley to her and her father, the same Mr. Knightley to all the world. . . . She would not marry, even if she were asked by Mr. Knightley" (*E* 416). Emma herself explains her reluctance to marry in terms of her attachment to her father. Earlier in the novel she tells Harriet Smith: "I believe few married women are half as much mistress of their husband's house, as I am of Hartfield; and never, never could I expect to be so truly beloved and important; so always first and always right in any man's eyes as I am in my father's" (*E* 84).

And, as we saw in chapter 3, even after Emma and Mr. Knightley have declared their love to each other, she is sufficiently swayed by her attachment to her father to resolve "of never quitting" him; and Mr. Knightley, understanding such feelings, is willing to sacrifice "a great deal of independence" to live uxorilocally at the Woodhouses' Hartfield (*E* 435, 449).

Just as the heroines' aberrant courtships question the presuppositions of romance, they also question the opposite notion of utilitarian eligibility. Without ignoring the utilitarian meaning of marriage, and fully aware of the discomforts of a small income, the heroines nonetheless refuse to allow signs of wealth and prestige to persuade them into conjugal bonds. Elizabeth Bennet rejects the proposal of Mr. Collins, though her best friend, Charlotte Lucas, quickly accepts his offer on the basis of its advantage. Elizabeth then rejects Darcy's first offer of marriage, in spite of the extraordinary greatness of the match from her perspective, and her refusal does not reflect a disregard for the pleasures afforded by wealth. Fanny rejects Henry Crawford's proposal—which, like Darcy's, is said to be "a little beneath him" (*MP* 292)—though her family and friends, finding her response "strange" and "more than they can understand," are tempted to conclude that Fanny is mad, her "understanding" temporarily "diseased" (*MP* 315, 352, 369). Elinor Dashwood marries Edward Ferrars, an eldest son of a wealthy family, but only after his mother legally defines him as her second son, thus forcing Edward to accept an unusually small living as a clergyman. Elinor is fully aware of economic realities when she accepts Edward's proposal of marriage, for she has had charge of her family's domestic economy following her father's death and has been critical of her sister's cavalier comments about the insignificance of wealth (*SS* 91).

Austen's heroines make decisions about marriage that fail to conform to the most generally held presuppositions about courtship, romance, advantage, and marriage itself. Frequently their fellow characters express surprise and bewilderment at their decisions. However, the heroines' marriages should be regarded not as antisocial behavior but, more appropriately, as alter-cultural. It is not that these marriages violate social rules, or even uniformly shared cultural conceptions; rather, they call into question the criteria which, in general, distinguish the category *marriageable* from the category *nonmarriageable*. Unlike the heroines' aberrant marriages, scandalous or antisocial behavior—for example, adultery, keeping a mistress, or jilting a poorer partner for a wealthier—is easily understood, precisely because it results from a hypertrophy of sensibility to either romance or advantage. Furthermore, the heroines' marital decisions cannot simply be attributed to enlightened self-interest, for while marriages selected on the basis of utility and/or romance lack mutual support and understanding, they do not necessarily lead to misery. Many characters—including Charlotte Lucas and Mr. Collins, and Sir Thomas and Lady Bertram—live contented and prosperous lives in empty marriages. The heroines' failure to subscribe to the conventional definitions of a desirable marriage reveals not a simple and sure formula for happiness but profound doubts about the appropriateness of identifying a marriage partner in terms of signs of romance and utility; that is, in terms of the conventions of courtship.

Alter-Culture Theory

Our notion of the alter-cultural should be compared to recent feminist readings of Austen, which we discussed briefly in chapter 1. Critics such as Newton (1981) and Poovey (1984) ask whether Austen, as a female voice within a patriarchal order, fully articulates liberation from gender domination. Not surprisingly, they find her only partially successful. To employ this interpretive frame is, in our view, to limit the identification of cultural resistance anachronistically to a politics that is visible and productive in the late twentieth century (cf. Cott 1987). Austen's valorization of what we have termed alter-cultural action is clearly not a specific program for ending patriarchy. Her texts encourage us to conceive human freedom less in terms of a singular, transhistorical model for a just social order than in terms of the value of rendering all social rules contingent and meaningful.

More generally, the discussion of alter-cultural marriages allows us to specify the relationships between several concepts that we have developed in the past chapters. We began by stressing the analysis of cultural variation. Rather than seeing the Austen texts as deriving from, or speaking about, some bounded entity—such as a social group (the English gentry circa 1800) or an individual (Jane Austen)—with a fixed and uniform conceptual system or culture, we approach them as presenting communication among characters who share some presuppositions and differ in their understanding of others. We suggested that concepts like *group* are reifications that hinder analysis of the context sensitivity and perspectival polysemy of communicative acts. In place of a discourse that posits a shared natural or social essence (such as blood or belief) of groups, we focus on the relationship of multiple interpretive frameworks in specific acts of communication. We have similarly avoided speaking of a hypostatized cultural system. Just as we eschew the term *group* to avoid privileging interactions in which actors affirm their solidarity, so too we do not use *culture* to privilege those concepts which are shared by some in some contexts. Though human experience is culturally constructed, it is not constructed in the form of singular, homogeneous cultures. Rather, we have argued, cultural concepts are manipulable ideas. Though recurring principles of association (such as the opposition between natural and constructed properties) can be traced through a set of interrelated concepts, it does not follow from this that the concepts form a mutually consistent, bounded set. Diverse messages are understandable to different actors with different points of view to the extent that actors' communicative logics have common underlying principles of organization. The relevant common features, then, vary from interaction to interaction, but as long as there are shared principles of understanding between two or more communicating parties, those parties can establish an area of mutual intelligibility and can communicate, to a relative degree, even about their differences. Thus the presence of shared principles allows for the interaction of differences and, as a consequence, for transformation and variation.

Following Jane Austen, we would oppose the reification of all social orders, whether those described by social scientists or those prescribed by social visionaries. As a social theorist, Austen the novelist offers us a countercurrent to the positivist visions of human society that otherwise emerged from nineteenth-century European observers of societies, cultures, and epochs.[5]

5. Our observations on feminist readings of Austen, with which we began this section, do not take into account the work of Morgan and Kneedler (1989), which was presented while our manuscript was in production. Morgan and Kneedler recognize many of the cultural transgressions of Fanny Price's marriage to Edmund Bertram, arguing that these transgressions make visible and contest the patriarchal order within which Austen lived. We share in much of their reading, particularly the recognition of the communicative thinness of courting civilities. "*Mansfield Park*," they write, "imagines love and passion as a friendly relation which has a reciprocity of mutual cooperation, knowledge, and communication—forms of affection that are both more loving and more personal than the codes of romantic love . . ." (5). We differ from Morgan and Kneedler in finding in Austen less a political critique of patriarchal oppression than an epistemological alternative to positivist social theory. Nonetheless, as we hint in our comparison of Austen and Rousseau in the next chapter, Austen's epistemological position does have political implications: it suggests a distrust of social engineering.

CHAPTER SIX

Creative Dance and the
Problem of Theatricality

The heroines' alter-cultural marriages are eminently creative acts precisely because they are structured in terms of new interpretations of material that is otherwise experienced as cliché. In this chapter we continue to move from an emphasis on the symbolic structure of the concepts of marriage and courtship to an emphasis on the characters' active manipulation of them, thus implicating a theory of cultural action and performance. From a slightly different perspective, we can describe this change in our emphasis as a shift from examining the problem of interpreting, or reading, the actions of others to the problem of producing messages for others to interpret. This approach to social analysis centers on the interaction among message-producing actors (between, for instance, characters in a text, between various readers and a text, or between an ethnographer and various natives) and does not presuppose that actors share a system of fixed and standard ideas, nor that they comprise integrated, bounded social groups. In sum, our analysis focuses on the characters' interactions as cultural action, that is, as performances that simultaneously make use of and comment on features of the characters' interpretive logics.

Human communication fundamentally contains the conditions for metacommunication; that is, communication or commentary about communication itself. For our present purposes it is useful to distinguish two types of metacommunication. First, every message communicates, at the very least, not only itself but the message producer's willingness to use communicative rules and understandings shared by some others. By using one form of speech or action rather than another (such as the dialect of genteel politeness), a speaker can claim to have a particular social status. Similarly, if the speaker's use of the code is not fluent, the claim can fail, even though the speaker manages to make the message itself understood. This complex feature of social messages is true of even the most ostensibly rule-governed aspects of social life. In Austen's novels, for instance, we find an elaborate code of etiquette that creates the appearance of relative uniformity of behavior amongst those of the genteel class, precisely because etiquette is used to represent and establish social status. It is not that social rules make everyone behave in the same way, but that behaving in a certain manner represents a particular status affiliation, and such representations may be successful or unsuccessful, appropriate or pretentious, socially cohesive or atomistic and divisive. Austen's characters constantly scrutinize others' use of communicative codes in order to assess their claims to relative social status.

A second type of metacommunication is practiced by Austen's protagonists, though not by her less self-conscious characters. The exemplary characters of Austen's novels are distinguished by their ability to discuss and analyze cultural conventions even as they participate in them. These characters use the metacommunicative aspect of language and culture to make visible, discuss, and play with their own social codes. In chapter 5 we saw how the heroines' courtships and marriages, taken as a set, implicitly comment on the most generally held conventions of marriage. In this chapter we carry the analysis further, moving to social activities in which the metacommunicative and creative aspects of cultural action are most explicit. We begin with dance, which is, as many of the characters recognize, a metaphor for both courtship and marriage; that is, a metaphor for the larger process of which it is so often a part, as well as for the telos of that process.

Dancing of and for Marriage

Courtship moves two people between two contrary states—from being unmarried (and perhaps being strangers) to being married and intimately attached. The gap between these two states is mediated not directly—not by a simple offer of marriage—but through a provisional and playful domain of conventionalized attentions, of which dancing is one of the most prominent. Indeed, dance is such a sure sign of courtship that it often stands for that process as a whole. "To be fond of dancing," according to the narrative of *Pride and Prejudice*, "was a certain step towards falling in love" (*PP* 9). And the narrative of *Mansfield Park* provides this discussion of the relationship of dancing to Maria Bertram and Mr. Rushworth's engagement: "After dancing with each other at a proper number of balls . . . an engagement . . . was entered into, much to the satisfaction of their respective families, and of the general lookers-on of the neighbourhood, who had, for many weeks past, felt the expediency of Mr. Rushworth's marrying Miss Bertram" (*MP* 39). That both the holding of dances and the dancing of partners are means of making marital matches is made clear by the significance, in the context of dancing, of four social distinctions: (1) between opposite-sex siblings and others of the opposite sex, (2) between women who are out and those who are not, (3) between persons who are married and those who are not, and (4) between women who are eligible and those who are spinsters. Dancing between brother and sister is something other than proper dancing. To recall a discussion from *Mansfield Park*, William Price tells his sister Fanny that it would be possible for them to dance together in Northampton since "nobody would know who I was here" (*MP* 250). Women do not attend dances until they have been presented to society. Married people may dance, but they need not; their dance activities serve primarily to facilitate the dancing of those who should dance—the young and marriageable. Married men not dancing with their wives are expected to offer themselves as partners to any unmarried women who have not been engaged for a particular dance, and married women often play the music for the dancing couples. Anne Elliot's sad slide toward spinsterhood is signaled by the fact that her friends have come to depend on her services as a musician for their dances, and when Captain Wentworth, newly reacquainted with her, inquires about her status as a dance partner, he is told that "she has quite given up dancing. She had rather play" (*P* 71–72).

As the causal antecedants of marriage, dance and other courting activities are, at one and the same time, marriagelike and not marriagelike: as models for making marriages, they are structured as metaphoric models of marriage without its finality and exclusiveness. Dance and courtship contain a manipulable mixture of the qualities of the inclusive relations amongst eligible status equals of the opposite sex and the exclusive relations of spouses. Thus courtship and dance combine qualities of the two social relations between which they mediate.

The similarities and differences between a dancing couple and a married couple are discussed explicitly by Henry Tilney and Catherine Morland, who speak as they dance together for the first time. Mr. Tilney deems dance "an emblem of marriage," to which Catherine responds with literalness that the lack of permanence and exclusivity between dancing partners makes an analogy between dance and marriage untenable: "But they are such very different things! . . . People that marry can never part, but must go and keep house together. People that dance, only stand opposite each other in a long room for half an hour." Henry responds by explaining the serious similarities, all in a manner that tweaks Catherine's earnestness:

> You will allow, that in both, man has the advantage of choice, woman only the power of refusal; that in both, it is an engagement between man and woman, formed for the advantage of each; and that when once entered into, they belong exclusively to each other till the moment of its dissolution; that it is their duty, each to endeavour to give the other no cause for wishing that he or she had bestowed themselves elsewhere, and their best interest to keep their own imaginations from wandering towards the perfections of their neighbours.

When Catherine insists on the difference, Henry continues his flirtation by playfully questioning Catherine's sense of constancy:

". . . may I not thence infer, that your notions of the duties of the dancing state are not so strict as your partner might wish? Have I not reason to fear, that if the gentleman who spoke to you just now were to return, or if any other gentleman were to address you, there would be nothing to restrain you from conversing with him as long as you chose?" (*NA* 76–78).

Thus Henry Tilney recognizes what Catherine denies and what their conversation, carried on while they dance, demonstrates: dancing occurs as a metaphor for marriage, and, as a result, dancing, both as an activity and as a topic of conversation, can serve as a way to play at and explore being a couple without the serious attachment of matrimony. Because dance is marriagelike without being marriage, it can serve as part of the process of producing marriages; that is, a process of selecting and rejecting possible partners. Henry and Catherine find out about each other as they exchange their views because they are taking part in an activity that simultaneously allows them playfully to be a couple and, doubly playfully, to talk about it.

While Henry Tilney's comments inform us about the ways in which an individual dance is like matrimony, Catherine Morland's comments, despite their naïvete, reveal how, if we take an evening of dancing as a unit, dancing is unlike matrimony. Henry points out that within a single dance a man and woman are a couple, but Catherine notes that these couples constantly separate and regroup throughout the evening. Thus Catherine's remarks make visible, beyond her own understanding, an important distance between dance and marriage. While Henry's view is clearly more subtle and informed than Catherine's, in Austen's texts it is the dialogue of both views that gives the fullest picture.

Taken together, Henry's and Catherine's views depict dancing as a sequence of episodes of particularity, or restricted exchange, within a larger frame of generalized exchange.[1] This framing context

---

1. Here, as in the previous chapter, we purposefully play with Lévi-Strauss's justly famous typology of marital exchanges (1969[1949]). Lévi-Strauss distinguishes between restricted exchanges (in which A gives and receives from B, and vice versa) and generalized exchanges (in which A receives from Z and

may thus be said to contain within it a multiplicity of potential relations of particularity. To court through dancing requires that characters markedly emphasize such particularity, in opposition to the rules of propriety, which dictate an obligation to dance with all potential spouses. Yet, dialectically, it is this ideal of inclusive exchange that allows the initiation and accentuation of particularity to occur in what is understood as a discreet and proper fashion.

The inclusive quality of exchange within an evening of dancing is evident in the social etiquette of choosing and accepting—that is, forming—dancing partners. A dance provides an acceptable means of being introduced to strangers. Wanting to dance with someone is considered good enough reason to find out his or her name or to arrange for a mutual acquaintance to make an introduction. At a public dance hall, such as the one described in Bath in *Northanger Abbey*, the master of ceremonies serves the purpose of introducing strangers. Introductions are both possible and expected at a dance, for within its framework all unmarried young adults of the same sex are paradigmatic equivalents. Because of this equivalence, much discretion is exercised over invitations to private dances, for the invitations construct a community of codancers and a community of potential spouses. Moreover, this equivalence of dancers may threaten those concerned to emphasize a status distinction. Thus Mr. Elton stops dancing under the pretext of being "an old married man [whose] dancing days are over" in order to snub Harriet Smith, leav-

---

gives to B, with no vice versa, only a circuit, or better, circulation). In an evening of dancing in Austen, persons (of both sexes) circulate around the room of potential spouses *as if* there was a rule of generalized exchange among the (exogamous) families gathered together. From the perspective of Lévi-Strauss's *Elementary Structures of Kinship*, however, Austen's characters carry out this generalized circuit of exchange at breakneck speed. Yet at the same time, each dancing couple is formed by a restricted exchange of partners, compliments, conversation, and so forth. This analysis suggests that what Lévi-Strauss isolates as distinct forms of 'elementary' systems of kinship are coeval aspects of courtship in Austen's 'complex' social world. Such forms are thus less distinct social types than recurring structures of *l'esprit humaine*, amenable to a dizzying variety of combinations.

ing her without a partner (*E* 327–28). Observing this, Mr. Knightley, who has not previously danced, steps in and offers Harriet a welcome invitation.

Knightley's response illustrates another way in which an evening of dance involves inclusive exchange. Though men, unlike women, have the independence to ask a partner to dance, this prerogative is not entirely free, for propriety dictates that men should obtain a partner and that no lady be neglected. To cite a second illustration of this point, Darcy's refusal to dance unless he is "particularly acquainted" with his partner (*PP* 11) quickly earns him a reputation for arrogance and thereafter undermines his attempts to use dance as a conventionalized code for initiating a courtship. When he asks Elizabeth to dance on subsequent occasions, his earlier behavior causes her to refuse him, in part because she doubts his real interest and in part because she wants to return his rejection.

Just as gentlemen should not leave any eligible ladies without partners, women's power of refusal also has qualities of inclusive exchange: when a woman not already engaged for the next dance wishes to refuse an invitation to dance, she must turn it down for a general reason rather than refuse a particular partner, and she must then give up dancing for the rest of the evening. Of course, women often make their decisions in terms of particular partners, but they must express and act on such decisions in the rhetorical form of a general principle. Thus, when Elizabeth Bennet refuses Mr. Darcy's surprising invitation to dance, she says, "I have not the least intention of dancing" (*PP* 26).

Whereas obligations to treat all potential partners equally give dancing a quality of inclusive exchange, other conventions of the dance allow the opposite quality of particularity. Courting through dance requires that this particularity, always present as a potential message of the dances within an evening of dancing, be made increasingly manifest. The characters in Austen's novels produce such messages of particularity through a number of rhetorical strategies. First, a man can express his particular attentions by asking a woman to dance with him prior to a ball's commencement, and specifically by asking for the first two dances (*MP* 268, 274; *PP* 87). Such an engagement is contingent on, and thereby signals, a preexisting and ongoing relationship between the partners. Moreover, it imposes greatly on a woman, for if it is refused, the woman is obliged not to dance during the entire evening. A man and a woman can also express particularity to each other by dancing together again and again, and thereby departing, to various degrees, from the etiquette of circulating among all potential spouses. The range of meaningful possibilities within this second idiom of particularity is illustrated, at least in part, by the dancing of Marianne and Willoughby in *Sense and Sensibility*, Jane and Bingley in *Pride and Prejudice*, and Maria and Rushworth in *Mansfield Park*.

At the beginning of *Sense and Sensibility*, Marianne and Willoughby devote themselves to each other with extreme particularity in the absence of an engagement, thereby leading to their "ridicule": "If dancing formed the amusement of the night, they were partners for half the time; and when obliged to separate for a couple of dances, were careful to stand together and scarcely spoke a word to any body else. Such conduct made them of course most exceedingly laughed at; but ridicule could not shame, and seemed hardly to provoke them" (*SS* 54). By contrast, Mr. Bingley shows his initial interest in Jane Bennet by asking her to dance twice, but he stays within the bounds of propriety by dancing with all the young ladies in the room. Thus Bingley uses a limited number of repeated dances to show particularity while honoring the etiquette of inclusive exchange. His actions nonetheless raise hopes (on the part of Jane, Elizabeth, and their mother), fears (on the part of Bingley's sisters and Darcy), and expectations (on the part of the neighborhood at large) that an engagement will be made between the dancing partners.

Finally, following her acceptance of Mr. Rushworth's proposal of marriage, Maria Bertram dances in an unrestricted fashion with other partners. Observing this, Rushworth's mother comments that the couple ought to be "excused from complying with the common forms" of circulating among all possible partners. To this, Maria's Aunt Norris responds that such "particularity" would be too blatant for Maria's "strict sense of propriety . . . [and her] true delicacy" (*MP* 117). Nonetheless, says Mrs. Norris, Maria's particular interest in Rushworth can be seen in the expression on her face when they dance together. Though Mrs. Norris is able to explain Maria's behavior in terms of the rules of etiquette, Maria's unrestricted dancing prefigures her subsequent infidelity. Thus the etiquette of particularity in courtship, like other communicative codes, is supple enough not only to represent but equally to misrepresent—not only to make matches but to unmake them.

Dancing Subtleties

The richest communication through dancing occurs between those characters, notably many of the heroines and their partners, who use the rhetoric of dance as a code for matrimony while simultaneously generating commentary about it. We have already examined Henry Tilney's complex dialogue with Catherine Moreland in which much more is exchanged than formal niceties. To cite a second example, Emma shows the creative potential of a code that generally seems, from the distance of late-twentieth-century America, rigid, formulaic, and inflexible. She shows that the metacommunicative aspect of cultural codes allows her to invert the social convention of men extending an invitation to dance without attacking that convention. When Mr. Knightley asks her with whom she is going to dance, Emma does not merely answer that she is unengaged but "hesitate[s] a moment" and responds, "With you, if you will ask me" (*E* 331). Thus she transgresses a rule of etiquette even as she perpetuates it. Their conversation continues in kind, with subtle messages of romantic interest communicated through a brief discussion of the presupposed cultural distinction between siblings and potential marital partners. Mr. Knightley begins by accepting Emma's offer, and she does likewise:

"Will you?" said he, offering his hand.

"Indeed I will. You have shown that you can dance, and you know we are not really so much brother and sister as to make it at all improper."

"Brother and sister! no, indeed." (*E* 331)

Finally, in *Pride and Prejudice* Elizabeth's and Darcy's powerful yet ambivalent mutual attraction is slowly and gropingly developed by a series of encounters not *of* but *about* dancing. At first Darcy refuses to dance with Elizabeth, then Elizabeth refuses Darcy; when they finally dance together, Elizabeth attempts to distance herself by talking about the talk that is proper between dancing partners:

> "It is *your* turn to say something now, Mr. Darcy.—*I* talked about the dance, and *you* ought to make some kind of remark on the size of the room, or the number of couples."
>
> He smiled, and assured her that whatever she wished him to say should be said.
>
> "Very well.—That reply will do for the present.—Perhaps by and bye I may observe that private balls are much pleasanter than public ones.—But *now* we may be silent."
>
> "Do you talk by rule then, while you are dancing?"
>
> "Sometimes. One must speak a little, you know." (*PP* 91)

In this passage Elizabeth emphasizes the formality of the conventions of dancing. She thereby makes use of dance as a courting exchange, but with complex inversion, to express her objection to a particular partner. With such explicit consciousness of her social conventions, Elizabeth Bennet warily and subtly, creatively and pragmatically, communicates with the conventions of her culture. Her recognition of that culture as something arbitrary and something that can be denied fits neatly James Boon's description of "professional anthropologists" and their "counterparts" elsewhere who "doubt the absoluteness of their own culture" and "displace the immediacy of their audience's social lives" (1982: 6).[2]

To summarize our argument to this point, the etiquette of dancing illustrates that conventions can generate a context for creativity as well as an unimaginative uniformity. Metaphors of and for marriage are about marriage but are not marriage itself; they can be richly interpreted and played with as well as facilely followed. We have suggested in this chapter and chapter 5 that Austen's exemplary characters do not naïvely reproduce courting conventions but implement a metapragmatic understanding of conventional codes *as codes*

---

2. Critic Tony Tanner (1986: 122–25) has borrowed Erving Goffman's idea of "role distance" to discuss Elizabeth's reflective cultural awareness.

to distance themselves from the process of courtship and, as a result, to gain some interpretive control over it. By contrast, other characters all too often allow themselves to be controlled by conventions, which thereby become, to borrow Edward Sapir's graphic description, "the dry rot of social habit, devitalized" (1949: 315).

The Austen texts thus ask us to go beyond the "of and for" of Kroeber and Kluckhohn (1963: 357) and Geertz (1973: 93–94). Geertz defined culture in terms of models "of" and "for" reality in a celebrated essay entitled "Religion as a Cultural System." There he argued that "unlike genes, and other non-symbolic information sources, which are only models *for*, not models *of*, culture patterns have an intrinsic double aspect: they give meaning, that is, objective conceptual form, to social and psychological reality both by shaping themselves to it and by shaping it to themselves" (1973: 93). Earlier, Kroeber and Kluckhohn had offered a related definition: "Culture consists of patterns . . . of and for behavior acquired and transmitted by symbols . . . culture systems may, on the one hand, be considered as products of action, on the other, as conditioning elements of further action" (1963: 357). In both discussions culture is understood as a given, and thereby something capable of providing people with conventional knowledge ("models of") and with routinized instructions for social action ("models for"). Neither definition bears on the issues of cultural creativity and social change. It is fitting, then, that Geertz has alluded to Austen in terms that suggest the conservative reading of Austen as champion of a well-ordered social world of the past: "Calculated politesse, outward form pure and simple, has there [i.e., Bali] a normative value that we . . . can scarcely, now that Jane Austen is about as far from us as Bali, any longer appreciate" (1973: 399).

Dramatic Sensibility

In our interpretation dancing is serious play; that is, a metaphor of matrimony that can lead to matrimony precisely because it is playfully unlike the restricted relationship of marriage. Using this interpretation as a point of departure, we turn to one of the thorniest problems in recent critical literature about Jane Austen—the heavily moralistic theatrical episode of *Mansfield Park*. As Lionel Trilling has written, "There is scarcely one of our modern pieties that [*Mansfield Park*] does not offend. . . . It scandalizes the modern assumptions about social relations, about virtue, about religion, sex, and art" (Trilling 1955: 185). He continues: "The great fuss that is made over the amateur theatricals can seem to us a mere travesty on virtue. And the more so because it is never made clear why it is so very wrong for young people in a dull country house to put on a play." In brief, Trilling argues that an understanding of this "seemingly absurd episode" is foreign to those who read Jane Austen now (191–92). Here we respond to Trilling by proposing an interpretation of this exotic episode based on our previous analysis of dancing and courtship.

The proposal to stage a private theatrical causes open disagreement among the young people of Mansfield Park. Tom Bertram, the elder son and—due to his father's extended visit to his estate in the West Indies—the nominal "master of the house" (*MP* 123), becomes enthusiastic about staging a theatrical after hearing his friend Mr. Yates discuss a similar project. The project also appeals to Tom's sisters, Maria and Julia, as well as to Henry Crawford and his sister, Mary, who have come to the Mansfield Park neighborhood for an extended visit to their half-sister, Mrs. Grant, whose husband has the church living at Mansfield Park. The foolish Mr. Rushworth, whose engagement to Maria Bertram awaits only Sir Thomas's approval upon his return, also joins the project. Only Edmund Bertram, Sir Thomas's younger son, and Fanny Price, the Bertrams' adopted cousin, object to the plan. Their objections are somewhat difficult to understand, not because Edmund and Fanny are reticent but because their judgments, as Trilling observes, presuppose commonsense assumptions about the theater different from our own. For instance, Edmund makes this attempt to dissuade Tom:

In a *general* light, private theatricals are open to some objections, but as *we* are circumstanced, I must think it would be highly injudicious, and more than injudicious, to attempt any thing of the kind. It would show great want of feeling on my father's account, absent as he is, and in some degree of constant danger; and it would be imprudent, I think, with regard to Maria, whose situation is a very delicate one. (*MP* 125)

And Tom replies:

You take up a thing so seriously! as if we were going to act three times a week till my father's return, and invite all the country. But it is not to be a display of that sort. We mean nothing but a little amusement among ourselves, just to vary the scene, and exercise our powers in something new. We want no audience, no publicity. We may be trusted, I think, in choosing some play most perfectly unexceptionable. (*MP* 125–26)

Edmund concludes his discussion with his brother by stating his belief that "my father would totally disapprove of it," but Tom disagrees. Edmund's conversations with his sisters are not reproduced in the text but are described as being equally unfruitful. Throughout these discussions, as well as Edmund's consultations with Fanny, who shares his disapproval, the objections to playacting and theatrical production are stated in terms of conventional propriety. The theatrical is disparaged with suspicions about the wild and ungenteel freedom of the theater which are presupposed, rather than explored, by the characters.

As the project develops, Tom's claim that the theatrical would be restrained and entirely proper is repeatedly belied: after protracted disputes the actors select a tawdry play, *Lover's Vows* (translated from a German play, *Child of Love*), that requires them to play scenes of lovemaking. Furthermore, the play becomes their major activity, and they rehearse repeatedly—much more than three times a week. Finally, the play requires a larger cast than they can provide, and they decide to bring in a comparative stranger from the neighborhood, thereby violating the privacy of the small circle of Mansfield Park society. In order to forestall this potential conversion of the drama into a public affair, Edmund decides, in spite of his strong objections, to participate in the play.[3] As they near their performance, Sir

3. Edmund's decision implicates not solely his sense of propriety but also his particular interest in protecting Mary Crawford from playing scenes of lovemaking with a stranger. It thus reveals his attraction to Miss Crawford, much to Fanny Price's dismay (*MP* 154–55).

Thomas returns unexpectedly to Mansfield Park, right in the middle of a rehearsal. That Tom and his sisters knew Edmund's account of Sir Thomas's opinion to be correct, in spite of their explicit claims to the contrary, is shown by their "consternation" and "horror" that Sir Thomas has found them rehearsing (*MP* 175). Moreover, Sir Thomas responds with strong disapproval and brings their production to a swift and certain end.

The amateur theatrical, like dancing, allows intimacy among unmarried ladies and gentlemen. Like dancing, the community of actors forms an inclusive set of equivalents: in spite of his strong objections to the theatrical, Edmund agrees to act in order to keep that community limited to the established social sphere of Mansfield Park. Furthermore, the young people select a play that intensifies the metaphoric association between the intimacy of acting together and the intimacy of courtship: they play at *Lover's Vows*. In its consequences the play does indeed produce romantic relationships— between Maria Bertram and Henry Crawford (who play and replay their scenes of lovemaking) and between Julia Bertram and Mr. Yates. Furthermore, these attachments are to varying degrees illicit. Maria is engaged to Mr. Rushworth during the planning and preparation of the theatrical, and she carries on her subsequent affair with Henry after her marriage. Julia later elopes with Mr. Yates, though this lesser impropriety is eventually forgiven. In addition, the rehearsals cause Edmund and Mary Crawford serious embarrassment because they must act scenes of love that make the ambiguities of their feelings for each other manifest. Fanny, though she steadfastly refuses to perform, is nonetheless painfully caught by watching Edmund read words of love to Mary.

In their playacting the characters neglect both the phatic conventions of courtship and the metaphors of and for marriage in their rehearsals. This neglect is an epitomizing instance of misplaced confidence in immediate appearance and, concomitantly, an abrogation of communicative and interpretive responsibility. Though the theatrical, as the characters have organized it, provides numerous foils for their various romantic interests, they treat it as a world of sheer play set apart from serious consequences. Ironically, they both insist that the play is no more than a diversion and are carried away by the romantic attachments they rehearse. This apparent contradiction between their words and their deeds results from taking experience too literally (the play is just a play) rather than literarily—that is, empirically rather than semiotically. Ostensibly the characters trivialize their playacting, though in practice they make too much of it—an ironic combination that stems from their failure to accept the connection between the theatrical and their lives outside the play. Forgetting that social action, even play, requires interpretive discernment, Henry and Maria, and Julia and Mr. Yates fall victim to the theatrical's illusions.

This instance of literalness has much in common with those courtships in which characters facilely follow the conventional rules of etiquette. To take the theatrical as mere play, or courting conventions as ensuring a good marriage, is in either case to neglect the relationship between a cultural code and what it is about. In the first case there is a denial that playacting can make something happen, and in the second there is excessive confidence in what a social code can do. In both cases there is a failure to recognize the code as a meaningful metaphor—no less and no more.

The denial in *Mansfield Park* of the serious pragmatics of playacting should be compared to two episodes of dance already discussed: the dialogue between Catherine Morland and Henry Tilney and that between Elizabeth Bennet and Fitzwilliam Darcy. Catherine denies the metaphoric relationship between dance and marriage, but her comments reflect a naïve inability to articulate the complexities of metaphoric relations rather than an intentional abrogation of communicative responsibility. Though Elizabeth actively and cleverly tells Darcy that their dancing is nothing but a formal play, her comments are not a denial of the relationship between dance and courtship. Rather, they self-consciously make use of that underlying relation in order to express Elizabeth's negative feelings about Darcy.

The dangers of privileging appearance—represented in *Mansfield Park* by the dangers of being carried away by the "representation" (121) of a tawdry, fictional world—is a recurring theme in Jane Austen's works. Characters are repeatedly misled by their prejudices or "first impressions" (to borrow from the original title of *Pride and*

Prejudice). These characters' moral education often involves learning to reinterpret initial impressions and to revise conclusions based
on them. As Tony Tanner has suggested, this conception of moral
education in Austen is related to the empiricist psychologies of
Locke and Hume. Both philosophers were concerned not only with
the origins of knowledge in sense impressions but with the psychological and social factors that influenced the interpretation of sensory data (Tanner 1986: 105–10). Though Austen was not an
empiricist, the epistemological concerns of eighteenth-century empiricism are central to her novels. Austen's heroines and heroes are
distinguished from less worthy characters by their willingness to
doubt the reliability of both sensory impressions and conventional
standards for interpreting them.

In Austen's texts, the failure to interpret, actively and provisionally, is common both to characters who explicitly follow the most
conventional wisdom and etiquette, on the one hand, and to those
who explicitly argue for the importance of immediate personal reactions and feelings, on the other. Indeed, not only do these extremes
commonly lack reflection and interpretation, but the distinction between them is questioned in the texts as well. Thus those characters
(notably Marianne Dashwood) who promote a romantic sensibility
of personal feeling repeatedly give voice to the most clichéd and
conventional views, and Austen's narratives repeatedly play with
this irony. For instance, Henry Tilney "lectures" Catherine Morland
on the principles of "picturesque" landscape drawing. When
Catherine eagerly agrees to Henry's aesthetic standards, he finds, as
the narrative playfully tells us, that Catherine has "a great deal of
natural taste" (*NA* 111). The disparity between what characters believe to be spontaneous judgment and what the text represents as
conventional wisdom is condensed in Austen's complex use of the
word *sensible*. Though this term generally refers to the capacity to
respond intensely to sense perceptions and sensations, Austen also
uses it to describe the practical (i.e., sensible) interest in "admin-
istering to the vanity of others" (*NA* 110–11). Thus in Austen's texts
the word *sensible* does double duty, covering both an excess of personal feeling and an excess of social agreement and reliance on common sense.

The need to recognize the complexities of messages—to use the rich potential of metacommunication in the construction of messages in order to communicate subtleties and specificities, and to interpret others with equal care—is insisted upon both by examples of interactions between Austen's characters and by the narratives' interactions with the reader. Throughout Jane Austen's novels it is dangerous for characters and readers alike to make judgments on the basis of first impressions. For instance, Elizabeth Bennet's quick judgments are characterized as prejudices, and Marianne Dashwood's errors result from her excess of sensibility; that is, the excessive intensity of her immediate responses to sense impressions or appearances. Marianne defends such reactions as spontaneous and honest, but they prove to be little more than unreflective reproductions of clichéd romantic sentiments. Her reactions are not highly personal feelings but merely simplistic and partial renderings of conventional wisdom. Similarly, the reader who only considers each moment of the novels as they occur in the narration will not fully understand them, for, as we show in chapter 7, reading and rereading—interpreting and reinterpreting—lead to different conclusions in Austen's texts.

Austen, Rousseau, and Theatricality

Rousseau, too, condemns theatricals, and he does so in a text that has, like Austen's, proved difficult for twentieth-century readers. Allan Bloom, who has provided the only English translation of *Lettre à d'Alembert sur les Spectacles*, sees Rousseau's argument as one instance of a transhistorical intra-European discourse on the need for political control of fictive arts (1968: xi–xxxiv). By contrast, David Marshall has provided a reading concerned more specifically with Rousseau's text, arguing that Rousseau objects not to fiction per se but to "theatricality":

> What Rousseau is focusing on . . . is the exchange of regards, the awareness of others as beholders that creates a theatrical consciousness. Rousseau's indictment of the acting and posing

that develop in society is not limited to a denunciation of deception, hypocrisy, or false representation. People become actors—and this acting is problematic—from the moment they are aware that they must represent themselves for others. (1986: 85)

As Marshall's argument suggests, Rousseau's critique of theater distills a more general critique of the symbolic foundation of social life. In *A Discourse on the Origin of Inequality*, for instance, Rousseau attributes what he sees as humanity's tragic fall from nature into society to the acquisition of language. Once humans were able to use symbolic categories to compare and judge one another, it "became the interest of men to appear what they really were not. To be and to seem became two totally different things; and from this distinction sprang insolent pomp and cheating trickery, with all the numerous vices that go in their train" ([1755] 1973: 86). For Rousseau, then, insincerity is the inevitable accompaniment of semiotic communication, and his critique of theatricality protests against the social determination of self. Thus, though Austen and Rousseau both condemn theatricals, their condemnations rest on profoundly different grounds. In *Mansfield Park* the theatrical does not stand for a fall from nature into society. Rather, the characters' rehearsals of *Lover's Vows* are an instance of a mistaken faith that social relations can be placed aside, bracketed, and escaped. Acting under this pretense of the discreteness of theater and society, the characters abrogate communicative responsibility. In Austen the theatrical is not a violation of self and nature but of social life. Whereas Rousseau's discussion of theater leads us to an imagined state of nature, Austen's insists on the inescapability of humanity's life in society.

This contrast between Rousseau and Austen is made even clearer if we examine Rousseau's descriptions of exceptional spectacles that overcome the problems of theatricality. Rousseau's *Lettre* provides two such examples, both—happily for our purposes—concerned with dances. One is a romanticized image of a state of nature; the other, a proposal for state regulation of romance and reproduction. The vision of natural harmony is, appropriately, recollected from Rousseau's childhood:

> The regiment of Saint-Gervais had done its exercises, and, according to the custom, they had supped by companies; most of those who formed them gathered after supper in the St. Gervais square and started dancing all together. . . . [T]he harmony of five or six hundred men . . . forming a long ribbon which wound around, serpent-like, in cadence and without confusion . . . could not be experienced coldly. It was late; the women were in bed; all of them got up. Soon the windows were full of female spectators who gave a new zeal to the actors; they could not long confine themselves to their windows and they came down; the wives came to their husbands, the servants brought wine; even the children, awakened by the noise, ran half-clothed amidst their fathers and mothers. The dance was suspended; now there were only embraces, laughs, healths, and caresses. There resulted from all this a general emotion that I could not describe but which, in universal gaiety, is quite naturally felt. . . .
>
> . . . After staying somewhat longer to laugh and chat in the square, they had to part, each withdrawing peaceably with his family; and this is how these lovable and prudent women brought their husbands back home, not in disturbing their pleasures but in going to share them. ([1758] 1968: 135–136, fn)

For Rousseau, the scene reconstitutes a state of nature: actions are spontaneous, behavior is uniform, pairings are perfect, and emotions are something language cannot describe. Unlike Austen's dances, there is no inappropriate flirtation, no misunderstanding, and no misjudged making of matches. There is, in short, only a functionalist restoration of nature's own society, the family.

Yet, as Marshall argues, "this utopian vision of an antitheatrical society is finally *not* advocated by Rousseau" as a response to the threat posed by D'Alembert's theater (97). Instead, for contemporary Geneva Rousseau proposes "balls for young marriageable persons" in which order is produced not by a state of nature but by state regulation:

All the false religions combat nature; ours alone . . . follows and regulates it. . . . [L]et me be instructed as to where young marriageable persons will have occasion to get a taste for one another and to see one another with more propriety and circumspection than in a gathering where the eyes of the public are constantly open and upon them, forcing them to be reserved, modest, and to watch themselves most carefully. . . . As for me, far from blaming such simple entertainments, I wish they were publicly authorized and that all private disorder were anticipated by converting them into solemn and periodic balls, open without distinction to all the marriageable young. *I wish that a magistrate, named by the council, would not think it beneath him to preside at these balls.* (128–29, emphasis added)

In Rousseau's vision the public gaze, backed by state power, will ensure sincerity and guarantee that communication will avoid ambiguity and remain transparent. In sum, as a matter of public policy, Rousseau advocates not a return to nature but a theater, regulated by society in the name of nature—which, says Rousseau, "[our religion] alone follows." Thus an image of a perfect, natural order serves as the antecedent for a call for order authorized by state power.

Ironically, then, in Rousseau—a figure often identified as a liberatory voice against modernity's routinization—we find a social theory that lays the foundation for an order of centralized domination; and in Austen, often relegated to a world of excessive formality, we find a voice for serious play. Rousseau understood that sociality and symbolic thought are inextricably linked, but he also mourned what he saw as the consequence of that linkage: that the ability to represent reality in symbolic terms was equally the ability to misrepresent it. This social theory led Rousseau in some places to reject society in favor of nature, and in others to champion totalitarianism in pursuit of a utopian order. By contrast, Austen advocated neither routinized social control nor a romantic escape from social responsibility. Her complex discourse shows not a formal world of tradition, well-integrated by powerful social rules and etiquette, but a complex, semiotically constructed and negotiated series of experiences that always allow and call for creative interpretation and reinterpretation. Such creativity can never be determined or reduced to a set of formal rules, precisely because it is made possible by rules that enable something to stand for something else without being that something else, and thus establish meaning and negation—propriety and transgression—together.

CHAPTER SEVEN

Narrating Multiple Realities

J ust as Austen's characters confront experiences that require them
to reinterpret their first impressions, so too do Austen's readers.
"Seldom, very seldom, does complete truth belong to any human
disclosure; seldom can it happen that something is not a little
disguised, or a little mistaken" (*E* 431). What better justification
than this characteristically noncategorical comment can there be for
the need to include the interrelations among multiple voices without
privileging any one of them with unassailable authority? Austen's
narrative techniques privilege multiplicity in and of itself. But her
use of multiplicity does not require unquestioning acceptance of all
opinions, nor a total relativism in which anything that anyone says
is true. Rather, it conveys a profound conviction that among competing opinions, assessments, and ideas, all possess significance because each can force a rereading of any other.

Whereas Jane Austen's novels demand rereading, ethnographies
do not. Like expository prose in general, they should contain no
ambiguities, no unsolvable problems that cannot be consigned to the
world beyond the text, there to await further research. Between the
covers of an ethnographic monograph the anthropologist-cum-
narrator possesses supreme authority. Relying on conventions of
ethnographic narration that facilitate the proper portrayal of exotic
realities, the anthropologist stakes "an unquestioned claim to appear

as the purveyor of truth in the text" (Clifford 1988: 25). The complexity of reported ethnographic fact may force readers to reread, but only to recapture forgotten details. Ethnographies are rarely constructed as polysemic messages that call for multiple and, above all, provisional interpretations.

Ethnographers have, of course, recognized the multiplicity of perspectives in social life and have included them within their narrative accounts. However, when multiple voices are introduced into ethnographic narration, they are usually framed and encompassed by an authoritative analytic voice, that of the Western natural scientist. For instance, George Stocking has shown how Malinowski intentionally introduces the individuated voices of natives into his text "'to convince . . . readers' that the ethnographic information offered them was 'objectively acquired knowledge' and not simply 'a subjectively formed notion'" (1983a: 105).[1] And in a discussion of *The Nuer*, James Clifford makes a similar argument about Evans-Pritchard's inclusion of native perspectives and multiple narrative voices to establish his "ethnographic authority" (1988: 32–34). In ethnographies multiple voices are orchestrated rather than interrelated, and the desired effect is unambiguous exposition and unprovisional analysis. Furthermore, readers of ethnographies expect and accept such decisiveness. Consider, for example, Edward Sapir's retrospective account of reading an ethnography in which authority was granted to an individual informant ("Two Crows"): "I remember being rather shocked than pleased when in my student days I came across such statements in J. O. Dorsey's 'Omaha Sociology' as 'Two Crows denies this'" (1949: 569).

In this chapter and the next we examine several aspects of Austen's narrative multiplicity and compare her narrative techniques to ethnographic writing and intercultural translation. We begin in this chapter with the microstructure of Austen's narrations, examining the interrelation of voices, not merely within a novel but within individual paragraphs and even sentences. Next we consider some ironies of plot and narrative exposition that ask readers to compare

1. The internal quotations are from the Bronislaw Malinowski Papers, British Library of Political and Economic Science, London School of Economics.

widely separated portions of the texts. Finally, we examine aspects of the overall structure of the novels, showing that at this level of organization, too, Austen's narrative techniques incorporate and explore the meaningful relations of diverse interpretive perspectives, thereby denying the possibility of any authoritative single reading.

The Narrative Relations of Contrastive Voices

Anthropologists use multiply voiced narration to convey unitary truths. Either corroborating witnesses are used to establish a single argument, or disagreement among informants becomes itself something to be explained. By contrast, in Jane Austen's narrations the interaction of multiple voices undermines the very possibility of unitary truth. Take, for example, Austen's narration of physical appearance, something that common sense tells us is a simple question of fact, perfectly amenable to treatment in an unambiguous descriptive language. As several critics have noted, Austen tells remarkably little about the physical appearance of her leading characters. More significantly, what Austen chooses to tell is narrated in relational rather than absolute terms; that is, we are told how particular characters appear *in the eyes of other characters* who are themselves concerned about their own appearances in relation to others.

As an example, consider a scene from *Mansfield Park* in which Fanny Price's attractiveness becomes a topic of discussion. Henry Crawford explains his libertine plan "to make Fanny Price in love with me" by claiming to his sister that Fanny's looks have greatly improved:

> You do not seem properly aware of her claims to notice. When we talked of her last night, you none of you seemed sensible of the wonderful improvement that has taken place in her looks within the last six weeks. You see her every day, and therefore do not notice it, but I assure you, she is quite a different creature from what she was in the autumn. . . . She must be grown two inches, at least, since October.

To which Mary Crawford replies: "Phoo! phoo! This is only because there were no tall women to compare her with, and because she has got a new gown, and you never saw her so well dressed before. She is just what she was in October, believe me. The truth is, that she was the only girl in company for you to notice, and you must have a somebody."

And when Henry goes on to confess to Mary that he has been unable to engage Fanny in flirtation, she revises her interpretation of Henry's evaluation of Fanny's improvement: "And so this is her attraction after all! This it is—her not caring about you—which . . . makes her so much taller, and produces all these charms and graces!" (*MP* 229–30).

In this discussion conflicting opinions about appearances (has Fanny truly improved?), as well as the motives for those opinions, are questioned, and there is no impartial viewpoint to which readers can appeal for certain judgment. Mary's suspicion that vanity is at the bottom of Henry's opinion is surely well founded. Henry's assertion that Fanny has grown two inches in six weeks is barely credible under any circumstances; Mary is undoubtedly right to point out the power of attractive clothing to elicit evaluations of personal charm credited to nature rather than artifice; and Mary must also be correct to assert that evaluations of height are always relative. Yet there are reasons to question Mary's argument. Other characters before Henry have remarked on Fanny's improvement and beauty (*MP* 178, 222). Moreover, because women who are out in society frequently envy or slight the attractions of their rivals, Mary's judgment with respect to Fanny cannot be accepted as impartial (cf. *MP* 44; *E* 23, 166–67). Significantly, the only descriptions of Fanny's appearance after the beginning of the novel (where the narrator describes Fanny as she looked at the age of ten [*MP* 12]) are those that come from points of view particular to characters who are not disinterested. There is no impartial narrator to give us an unbiased account.

Austen's use of the multiple perspectives of interacting characters to convey a range of interpretations is not confined to such obviously subjective questions as that of physical attractiveness. Even neutral events are often constructed in the novels out of markedly different points of view. Consider this apparently unproblematic narration of a simple event, the moment of reunion of Fanny Price and her sailor brother:

. . . scarcely ten days had passed since Fanny had been in the agitation of her first dinner visit, when she found herself in an agitation of a higher nature—watching in the hall, in the lobby, on the stairs, for the first sound of the carriage which was to bring her a brother.

It came happily while she was thus waiting; and there being neither ceremony nor fearfulness to delay the moment of meeting, she was with him as he entered the house, and the first minutes of exquisite feeling had no interruption and no witnesses, unless the servants chiefly intent upon opening the proper doors could be called such. This was exactly what Sir Thomas and Edmund had been separately conniving at, as each proved to the other by the sympathetic alacrity with which they both advised Mrs. Norris's continuing where she was, instead of rushing out into the hall as soon as the noises of the arrival reached them. (*MP* 233)

The passage begins with the narrator working through Fanny's consciousness, and we see a scene as constructed by the agitation of a timid yet feeling personality. Briefly we are asked to imagine what the scene might look like to servants who must suppress all signs of human feeling. Then we are told of Sir Thomas's and Edmund's attempts to orchestrate the reunion by ensuring its privacy and, finally, of the officious and insincere Mrs. Norris's desire to play a leading role in it. In Austen's narrations, then, apparently unitary events do not merely happen: the purposeful actions of many characters contribute to any outcome, and, moreover, those characters often construe a single event in noticeably different terms.

As a final, more extended, example of the capacity of Austen's narratives to weave together multiple aspects of social reality, consider the first chapter of *Pride and Prejudice*, which begins:

It is a truth universally acknowledged, that a single man in possession of a good fortune, must be in want of a wife.

However little known the feelings or views of such a man may be on his first entering a neighbourhood, this truth is so well fixed in the minds of the surrounding families, that he is considered as the rightful property of some one or other of their daughters. (*PP* 3)

Austen opens *Pride and Prejudice* with a parody of an aphorism—a somewhat dubious statement that undercuts itself through excessive certainty, thereby becoming what Bakhtin (1981) terms "double-languaged." The narrative voice hints that people delude themselves by believing that wealthy bachelors inevitably need and desire wives. The hint may or may not be visible on first reading, but its potential ironies are developed thereafter. The second sentence separates the narrative voice from received wisdom and specifies that the truism is an opinion firmly held by a neighbourhood of families with daughters, no matter how little the neighbors know of the bachelor. Thus the belief that wealthy bachelors need and want wives is doubly undermined. First, it is no longer a universal view but a view held by neighbors with little knowledge and implicitly questioned by a more knowing narrator. Second, it is represented as a belief motivated by familial interest rather than a dispassionate assessment of experience.

The rest of the chapter—save the last paragraph—is a dialogue between the master and mistress of one such family, the Bennets, in one such neighborhood. In their discussion Mrs. Bennet reveals herself as someone whose views of a wealthy bachelor are indeed colored by her devotion to the project of marrying off her daughters, and Mr. Bennet teases his wife, ironically questioning her understanding of an unknown bachelor as well as of the conventions of visiting and courtship:

> "My dear Mr. Bennet," said his lady to him one day, "have you heard that Netherfield Park is let at last?"
>
> Mr. Bennet replied that he had not.
>
> "But it is," returned she; "for Mrs. Long has just been here, and she told me all about it."
>
> Mr. Bennet made no answer.
>
> "Do you want to know who has taken it?" cried his wife impatiently.
>
> "*You* want to tell me, and I have no objection to hearing it."
>
> This was invitation enough.

"Why . . . Mrs. Long says that Netherfield is taken by a young man of large fortune from the north of England; . . . that he is to take possession before Michaelmas, and some of his servants are to be in the house by the end of next week."

"What is his name?"

"Bingley."

"Is he married or single?"

"Oh! single, my dear, to be sure! A single man of large fortune. . . . What a fine thing for our girls!"

"How so? how can it affect them?"

"My dear Mr. Bennet," replied his wife, "how can you be so tiresome! You must know that I am thinking of his marrying one of them."

"Is that his design in settling here?"

"Design! nonsense, how can you talk so! But it is very likely that he *may* fall in love with one of them, and therefore you must visit him as soon as he comes."

"I see no occasion for that. You and the girls may go, or you may send them by themselves, which perhaps will be still better, for as you are as handsome as any of them, Mr. Bingley might like you the best of the party."

"My dear, you flatter me. . . . But consider your daughters. Only think what an establishment it would be for one of them. Sir William and Lady Lucas are determined to go, merely on that account, for in general you know they visit no new comers. Indeed you must go, for it will be impossible for *us* to visit him, if you do not."

"You are over scrupulous surely. I dare say Mr. Bingley will be very glad to see you; and I will send a few lines by you to assure him of my hearty consent to his marrying which ever he chuses of the girls; though I must throw in a good word for my little Lizzy."

"I desire you will do no such thing. Lizzy is not a bit better than the others; and I am sure she is not half so handsome as Jane, nor half so good humoured as Lydia. But you are always giving *her* the preference."

"They have none of them much to recommend them," replied he; "they are all silly and ignorant like other girls; but Lizzy has something more of quickness than her sisters." (*PP* 3-5)

Thus far, then, the narration has established and related two opposing points of view while moving from the general level of universal truths to the local level of specific characters. In the first paragraph of the chapter a belief about wealthy bachelors is expressed initially in the voice of general conviction, the "truth universally acknowledged" by an unspecified public and simultaneously challenged by a narrator's irony.[2] In the second paragraph the initial opinion about wealthy bachelors is attributed to neighborhood families, particularly those with daughters, and again challenged by a narrator as well as by the hypothetical wealthy man, who has, perhaps, views of his own. And in the conversation cited immediately above, each position is voiced by one character, Mrs. or Mr. Bennet, and then challenged by the other. Thus these paired viewpoints are presented at different levels of generality, and their sequence, from general to particular, moves us energetically into the world of the characters—a world that we can take as a merely reported, neutrally presented world only if we read naïvely and overlook the various interpretive dialogues that link readers to text to narrator to characters.

The existence of two points of view, expressed at three levels of generality, does not, however, exhaust dialogue and diversity in the first chapter. At the intermediate level of the second paragraph, each apparently unitary viewpoint contains a potential for discord. The families of a given neighborhood may indeed share a sanguine view of the likelihood of a new conjugal bond, but they will likely differ

2. Here "simultaneously" is to be taken literally. As Bakhtin points out, the comic novelist's irony is often expressed within the same sentence, and by the same words: "Another's speech . . . is [not] clearly separated from authorial speech. . . . This varied *play with the boundaries of speech types*, languages and belief systems is one of the most fundamental aspects of comic style" (1981: 308). While we adopt the concept of dialogic from Bakhtin, we differ in finding such narration in texts as uncarnivalesque as Jane Austen's.

about which of their daughters should join the wealthy bachelor. Being "the rightful property of some one or other" of the young women, the bachelor can belong rightfully to one only; hence the likelihood of rivalry and dispute. Similarly, the narrator's challenge to popular opinion about bachelors is itself vulnerable to challenge. By emphasizing that particular bachelors are likely to have views of their own, the narrator establishes the possibility that the bachelor, when known, might call into question the narrator's own authority. The feelings of this inchoate character may, by the novel's end, ironize the narrator's irony, for any specific bachelor may indeed be in want of a wife. The reader cannot predetermine the implications of the narrator's initial irony—further ironies may unfold.

At the next level, that of the characters specific to *Pride and Prejudice*, the potential for discord among adherents to received wisdom concerning bachelors is manifest in Mrs. Bennet's suspicions about those whom she views as rivals: Mrs. Long and Lady Lucas. Furthermore, the voice of irony and challenge (Mr. Bennet) is itself marked as provisional and incomplete through a marked shift in the narrator's introduction of this character. In contrast to Mrs. Bennet, who is introduced in unmarked fashion (quoted and framed speech ["'My dear Mr. Bennet,' said his lady to him"]), Mr. Bennet's introduction presents him at first in muted voice (indirect quotation ["Mr. Bennet replied that he had not"]), then speechless ("Mr. Bennet made no answer"), and then faceless (direct but unframed quotation), thereby representing him as someone distant both from his wife and from the narration that presents the characters to the readers. Indeed, we discover as we read the novel, Mr. Bennet's awareness of other characters' silliness and self-deception has led him away from communication and social responsibilities, and into the self-deceptive seclusion of his library.

The dialogue of truism and skepticism between Mr. and Mrs. Bennet bears on more than the initial wisdom about wealthy bachelors. In his responses to his wife Mr. Bennet transgresses sociolinguistic rules, refusing normal conversational cues ("Mr. Bennet made no answer" and "*You* want to tell me, and I have no objection to hearing it"), and playfully denies the need to follow established conventions of neighborly visiting and courtship. Knowing his wife's gullibility, Mr. Bennet seeks to shock her by suggesting that he will send a note to Mr. Bingley that deals explicitly with the possibility of marrying one of his daughters. Here Mr. Bennet's humor depends on and calls attention to the disjunction between the universal interest in marrying a daughter to Mr. Bingley and the respect for social conventions requiring such desires to be communicated obliquely. Similarly, Mr. Bennet's commitment to teasing and mockery raises absurd, but nonetheless possible, alternatives to established conventions of courtship and attractiveness: "You and the girls may go, or you may send them by themselves, which perhaps will be still better, for as you are as handsome as any of them, Mr. Bingley might like you the best of the party."

Finally, in this brief dialogue between Mrs. and Mr. Bennet, Austen has meticulously inscribed, among others, the following four social divisions and distinctions, and hence social alternatives:

1. Mrs. Bennet's description of the renting of Netherfield shows that master and servant are distinguished in conversation as those worthy of being named and those who remain nameless. Mrs. Bennet names neither master nor servant, but her husband's request for further information concerns only the master, passing over the servants as though they did not exist: "he is to take possession before Michaelmas, and some of his servants are to be in the house by the end of next week."
   "What is his name?"
   "Bingley."

2. The spouses' quibbling over which of their children should be preferentially presented to Mr. Bingley suggests not only sibling rivalry but the rivalry of parents who competitively champion different children. Such rivalries show that there can be disagreement within families as well as between them.

3. Mr. Bennet favors his daughter Lizzy because of her intelligence, but Mrs. Bennet prefers Jane for her beauty and Lydia for her good humor. Here the narrative broaches the possibility of difference over the evaluations of particular women, as well as difference in the standards used to evaluate them.

4. Mr. Bennet contends that girls are "all silly and ignorant," a remark that implicitly contrasts women to men and thereby suggests the presence of diversity stemming from sharply differentiated gender roles.

As these four examples show (and one could find others), even in narrating a routine conversation, Austen's texts richly draw upon and open up an array of social distinctions, any one of which might motivate major disagreements in other interactional contexts. Even when unity and agreement are explicit and manifest, fractionating possibilities are inherent in the complexities of Austen's narration of social realities.

In the final paragraph (preceded by additional dialogue not discussed here) an impersonal narrator appears to comment authoritatively on the principal characters presented:

> Mr. Bennet was so odd a mixture of quick parts, sarcastic humour, reserve, and caprice, that the experience of three and twenty years had been insufficient to make his wife understand his character. *Her* mind was less difficult to develope. She was a woman of mean understanding, little information, and uncertain temper. . . . The business of her life was to get her daughters married; its solace was visiting and news. (*PP* 5)

Here is the same voice of irony that we saw at the outset, directed this time at the personal failings of the characters. Moreover, most readers would agree that these observations are as objective as any expressed in the novel; the subsequent actions of Mr. and Mrs. Bennet bear out the narrator's initial description of their characters. Yet the narrative's dominant voice of irony does not itself remain unitary. The ironic first sentence of the first chapter can be called into question by a complete reading of the novel—for as *Pride and Prejudice* and Austen's other novels show, wealthy bachelors characteristically *do* desire wives. Though the narrator's ironical questioning of universal truths still stands, that initial irony is in turn undercut by the outcome of the novel: public opinion, the neighborhood, and Mrs. Bennet turn out to have been correct in their assessment of the unknown bachelor's feelings or views, and his successful courtship of a neighborhood daughter ultimately belies the narrator's smugness.[3]

Moreover, the authority of the narrative voice of *Pride and Prejudice* is further questioned if we locate the novel within the larger context of Austen's oeuvre. Not only is the narrative of Austen's next published work, *Mansfield Park*, essentially devoid of irony, but the characters within it who are possessed of quick and ironic wit are ultimately untrustworthy. If *Pride and Prejudice* suggests that irony and charm are to be taken as signs of narrative authority and personal merit, that suggestion is challenged by *Mansfield Park*'s thoroughgoing exorcism of these traits. So, too, *Emma* might be read as establishing the provisionality of *Mansfield Park*'s religiosity and moral seriousness—as might *Pride and Prejudice*, retrospectively. To give a final example, *Persuasion* might be read as contesting the reproduction of social hierarchy that follows from the plot of *Emma*. In general, rather than reading Austen's oeuvre in terms of some unifying principle of closure, we suggest that each novel be read as speaking against the completeness of the others.

Rereading Misreadings

We suggested above that the interpretive caution necessary to Austen's readers parallels the interpretive skills that Austen requires of

---

3. For another close reading of the opening chapter of *Pride and Prejudice* consult Van Ghent (1953: 99–103). Following Schorer (1952), Van Ghent stresses the discrepancy between the determinative power of property relations in Austen's world and the struggle of the author's economically powerless heroines to find space for their individuality within that despotic social order. Because her reading is grounded in economic determinism, it is not surprising that Van Ghent ignores the ironized irony of the novel's initial sentence. She recognizes that the first sentence ironically conveys its opposite—"a single woman must be in want of a man with a good fortune" (100)—but overlooks the opposite of the opposite ironically suggested by the outcome of the novel. For a reading that similarly reduces Austen's irony see Armstrong (1987: 135). Armstrong differs from Van Ghent, however, in that she reductively analyzes the irony of the opening of *Pride and Prejudice* with respect to gender concepts rather than economic circumstances.

her leading characters. Those characters often find themselves mistaken in prior assessments of a situation and must learn to suspect first impressions and implicit prejudices. The ease with which well-intentioned characters can misread a simple event is illustrated when Mrs. Jennings partially overhears a serious conversation between Colonel Brandon and Elinor Dashwood. Mrs. Jennings is a woman who, having married off two daughters, "had now therefore nothing to do but to marry all the rest of the world" (*SS* 36), and since the midpoint of the novel she has suspected matrimonial interest between Elinor and the Colonel (*SS* 216). Thus when Colonel Brandon follows Elinor to a secluded area of Mrs. Jennings's sitting room "with a look of particular meaning, and conversed with her there for several minutes," Mrs. Jennings is convinced that he is proposing:

> The effect of his discourse on the lady too, could not escape her observation, for though she was too honourable to listen . . . she could not keep herself from seeing that Elinor changed colour, attended with agitation, and was too intent on what he said, to pursue her employment.—Still farther in confirmation of her hopes . . . some words of the Colonel's inevitably reached her ear, in which he seemed to be apologizing for the badness of his house. This set the matter beyond a doubt. She wondered indeed at his thinking it necessary to do so;—but supposed it to be the proper etiquette. (*SS* 281)

As Mrs. Jennings soon learns, however, the Colonel is merely asking Elinor to convey an offer of patronage to her brother-in-law, Edward Ferrars, who has been disinherited for refusing to renounce an engagement that has become publicly known (*SS* 292). Elinor's embarrassment stems from her matrimonial interest in Edward, not the Colonel, and Mrs. Jennings easily, if foolishly, misreads a conversational exchange that seems to contain signs of a courtship encounter. Mrs. Jennings is even able to imagine the possibility of a convention unknown to her in order to account for Colonel Brandon's apologetic remark about "his house." However, the house in question is that connected with the church living that the Colonel will offer Edward, not the Colonel's own house, as Mrs. Jennings thought.

Not only events but personal appearance—those bundles of physical attributes presumed to belong unambiguously to particular individuals—are shown in the texts to be subject to multiple and mutable (mis-)readings that can interact over time. We have already examined a disputed claim concerning Fanny Price's beauty; now let us consider a similar interpretive problem that endures not for a scene but throughout an entire novel, *Persuasion*, in which disputed evaluations of Anne Elliot's physical appearance are closely connected to the unfolding of the plot.

Persuasion begins with a description of Anne's father, Sir Walter Elliot, who is portrayed as excessively vain and foolishly infatuated with his own good looks and his place in society: "He considered the blessing of beauty as inferior only to the blessing of a baronetcy; and the Sir Walter Elliot, who united these gifts, was the constant object of his warmest respect and devotion" (*P* 4). We learn also that Sir Walter favors his eldest daughter, Elizabeth, who has absorbed his prejudices, and that he considers Anne and a third daughter to be "of very inferior value" (*P* 5). With this information as background, the reader is treated to the following description of the heroine: "A few years before, Anne Elliot had been a very pretty girl, but her bloom had vanished early; and as even in its height, her father had found little to admire in her (so totally different were her delicate features and mild dark eyes from his own); there could be nothing in them now that she was faded and thin, to excite his esteem" (*P* 6).

This description of Anne begins as a narrator's statement of fact. As part of the novel's opening, it thus appears as a realistic setting of character and scene. Yet as the passage proceeds, the narrative's disinterested voice increasingly yields to one interested perspective—that of Sir Walter, who, we are told, found little to admire in Anne even when she was in bloom. Moreover, we are also told of the subjective basis for Sir Walter's judgment: he cannot appreciate beauty different from his own. Thus by the end of the passage the narrator has destroyed any pretense of the objectivity of this description, though the language remains realistic throughout.

Return now to the description of Anne Elliot and consider the temporal implications of the idea of bloom. This naturalistic metaphor can indicate a condition that is either singular or cyclical. What has bloomed once might, or might not, bloom again: some flowers bloom only once, others return from dormant winters. Sir Walter believes that his second daughter's bloom is gone forever. However, as the novel proceeds, Anne Elliot begins to bloom again:

> When they came to the steps . . . a gentleman at the same moment preparing to come down, politely drew back, and stopped to give them way. They ascended and passed him; and as they passed, Anne's face caught his eye, and he looked at her with a degree of earnest admiration, which she could not be insensible of. She was looking remarkably well; her very regular, very pretty features, having the bloom and freshness of youth restored by the fine wind which had been blowing on her complexion, and by the animation of eye which it had also produced. It was evident that the gentleman, (completely a gentleman in manner) admired her exceedingly. Captain Wentworth looked round at her instantly in a way which shewed his noticing of it. (*P* 104)

Here the narrator insists that bloom is a function of context and social relations. Anne Elliot's bloom comes from the effects of weather on particular aspects of her countenance—her complexion and eyes. Moreover, for Captain Wentworth, Anne's bloom depends also on the fact that a third person notices it—and the narrator takes care to specify that the social condition of that third person, his genteel status, is not without influence on Wentworth's reaction.

Captain Wentworth is the hero of *Persuasion*. At the time of Anne Elliot's first bloom, seven years before the novel takes place, she had broken an engagement to him. *Persuasion* is the story of Wentworth's return to her. When they first renew their acquaintance, Anne is told by her sister of Wentworth's initial judgment of her:

> "Captain Wentworth is not very gallant by you, Anne, though he was so attentive to me. Henrietta asked him what he thought of you, . . . and he said, 'You were so altered he should not have known you again.'" . . .
>
> Frederick Wentworth had used such words . . . but without an idea that they would be carried round to her. He had

thought her wretchedly altered, and, in the first moment of appeal, had spoken as he felt. He had not forgiven Anne Elliot. (*P* 60–61)

Once again, in this passage realism is undercut by the narrative's insistence that observations are a function of the relationship between observer and observed, for Wentworth's perception is traced to his having "not forgiven Anne."

As we have seen, Wentworth learns over time to reevaluate Anne Elliot. Indeed, at the end of the novel, when the lovers are reunited, Wentworth assures Anne that his opinion of her appearance had never wavered, citing a conversation with his brother as proof:

"I was six weeks with Edward," said he, "and saw him happy. . . . He enquired after you very particularly; asked even if you were personally altered, little suspecting that to my eye you could never alter."

Anne smiled, and let it pass. It was too pleasing a blunder for a reproach. It is something for a woman to be assured, in her eight-and-twentieth year, that she has not lost one charm of earlier youth: but the value of such homage was inexpressibly increased to Anne, by comparing it with former words, and feeling it to be the result, not the cause of a revival of his warm attachment. (*P* 243)

Here Jane Austen's narrative epistemology is made explicit: the state of a social relationship is said to condition, not follow from, the facts of physical appearance. It is a position that Austen wanted to stress, as is shown by comparison with an earlier draft of the novel's conclusion. In the unused version we are told only that Wentworth "assured [Anne] that—(so far from being altered for the worse!), she had gained inexpressibly in personal Loveliness" (*P* 264). In this version the narrator does not explicitly remind the reader of Wentworth's earlier criticism of Anne's looks; but when Jane Austen rewrote the scene, she insisted on the contrast between his earlier and later opinions, thereby stressing the connection between apparently neutral descriptions and the state of mind of the observer. Southam suggests that in the earlier version, in contrast to the later, Anne and

Wentworth lack "a full understanding of the past" (1986a: 322). In our reading, however, Austen's narration precludes any such full understanding (just as it precludes truth universally acknowledged), and the final version emphasizes Wentworth's selective reconstruction of his own past perception of Anne's appearance. Moreover, though Wentworth's reconstruction does not represent Southam's "full understanding of the past," it does suggest an acquisition of wisdom befitting the novel's end, since it indicates the strength of his renewed commitment to Anne.

In Austen's view, then, there is no single authoritative perspective from which to learn what a person's physical nature really is. Multiple readings, as well as an awareness of the provisionality of any one reading, are always desirable. Austen is even more concerned to make such arguments with respect to her characters' intellectual, moral, and social qualities. In *Northanger Abbey* Catherine Moreland is carried away by her "infatuation" for gothic romances; she allows "visions of romance" and "an imagination resolved on alarm" to dominate her interpretation of life at General Tilney's family seat, Northanger Abbey, only to find that such interpretations confound her attempts to understand "human nature . . . in the midland counties of England" (*NA* 199–200). To her embarrassment, Catherine's fanciful suspicions concerning the General's gothic crimes are discovered and disproven; at the same time, she fails to understand a more commonplace failing—mercenary ambition—that would account for the General's ambivalence toward her.

In contrast to Catherine's literal literary misreadings, Emma is so eager to construe courting behavior in terms that satisfy her egocentric and snobbish vision of the social order that she seriously misinterprets both Mr. Elton and Frank Churchill, with unhappy consequences for herself and her friends. In both cases Emma, like Mrs. Jennings, responds to certain conventions expressing particularity but mistakes the person to whom it is addressed. Throughout several chapters Emma misreads Mr. Elton's attentions to herself, thinking them to be directed to her protégée, Harriet Smith. For example, when Emma suggests that she attempt a portrait of Harriet, Mr. Elton responds with a suitor's admiration for Emma's artistic accomplishments:

"Let me entreat you," cried Mr. Elton; "it would indeed be a delight! Let me entreat you, Miss Woodhouse, to exercise so charming a talent in favour of your friend. I know what your drawings are. How could you suppose me ignorant? Is not this room rich in specimens of your landscapes and flowers; and has not Mrs. Weston some inimitable figure-pieces in her drawing-room, at Randalls?"

Yes, good man!—thought Emma—but what has all that to do with taking likenesses? You know nothing of drawing. Don't pretend to be in raptures about mine. Keep your raptures for Harriet's face. (*E* 43)

Here Emma almost willfully misinterprets Mr. Elton, so convinced is she of the appropriateness of a match between him and Harriet. Mr. Elton's courtship of Emma continues, and Emma continues to presume that his object is Harriet, despite Mr. Knightley's warning that Mr. Elton "does not mean to throw himself away" on Harriet (*E* 66), and despite Mr. John Knightley's suggestion that Elton is addressing himself to Emma (*E* 112). Only after Mr. Elton proposes to her does Emma realize the degree to which she has misinterpreted his feelings, but even then she is as much inclined to blame Elton, for "having the arrogance to raise his eyes to her," as herself (*E* 135-36).

Only partially chastised, it is not surprising that Emma commits a similar error concerning Frank Churchill. Even before she meets him, "she had frequently thought . . . that if she *were* to marry, he was the very person to suit her" (*E* 119). Thus she is fully prepared by her own fancy to misinterpret Frank Churchill's ambiguous behavior toward herself. Emma suspects that he loves her (*E* 262) but later learns that his flirtation with her was designed to cover up his secret engagement to Jane Fairfax (*E* 441).

Many readers, though lacking Emma's self-interested position, will nonetheless similarly misconstrue the ambiguities of Frank Churchill's behavior. Some may even follow Emma in her over-determined interpretation of Mr. Elton's behavior to her and Harriet. But even for those who guess correctly during a first reading, re-reading will cast the characters' interactions and the novel's events in a new light: what was before awkward or confusing now becomes ironic. Some readers have criticized Austen's use of secret knowledge—Frank Churchill's hidden engagement, for example—to manipulate her readers' relationship to the plot. As Wayne Booth puts it, "One objection to this selective dipping into whatever mind best serves our immediate purposes is that it suggests mere trickery and inevitably spoils the illusion of reality." Booth goes on to defend Austen from such charges, claiming that the author cares about both "mystery" and "irony," two "effects" which exclude each other in a single reading and thus demand multiple readings. Nonetheless, Booth suggests that Austen's use of "mere mystification" is "perhaps the weakest aspect" of *Emma* (1961: 254–55). By contrast, we argue that the use of such literary conventions as mystery and irony to force rereading not only does not spoil the illusion of reality but teaches an understanding of reality that is both sociologically and semiotically sophisticated.

Because "complete truth" (*E* 431) is unattainable in the analysis of social life, each of Austen's novels demands rereading. The apparently ludicrous universal truth that is introduced and ironically undercut at the beginning of *Pride and Prejudice* turns out to apply to the wealthy, unmarried gentlemen in the novel, and readers are reminded that they must question the authority of even an ironic and worldly-wise narrator. Similarly, when the heroine of the same novel refuses Mr. Collins and asks him not to interpret her refusal as conventional feminine wile—because "I do assure you that I am not one of those young ladies (if such young ladies there are) who are so daring as to risk their happiness on the chance of being asked a second time" (*PP* 107)—readers can only construe the event in a straightforward manner. Collins's "stupidity" (*PP* 122) and Elizabeth's intelligence would seem to preclude irony or any other alternative reading of the lady's remark. Yet Elizabeth ultimately finds that her happiness will depend on Mr. Darcy's willingness to make her a second offer, and indeed, that this second offer is more acceptable, in part, because of Darcy's positive, constructive reaction to her prior rejection. Thus Austen's texts continually show us that alternative perspectives can change the meaning even of those events and truths that seem most unambiguous. Retrospectively,

Elizabeth's comment is ironized, and a seemingly simple statement is shown to be not false, but more complicated than we first imagined.

Endings and Narrative Ratios

Each of Austen's novels closes with the pronouncement of a blissful marriage for the heroine whose fate has served as the focus of the novel. Yet the narrative undermines the credibility of these conclusive pronouncements. Most obviously, there is Austen's ironic hyperbole: "To begin perfect happiness at the respective ages of twenty-six and eighteen, is to do pretty well" (*NA* 252), and "the wishes, the hopes, the confidence, the predictions of the small band of true friends who witnessed the ceremony, were fully answered in the perfect happiness of the union" (*E* 484). Furthermore, two other elements of the narrative structure reveal the problematic quality of even the heroines' promising marriages. First, each alliance brings the plot to an abrupt close. Second, the success of each heroine's married life is described with only a few words, contrasting sharply with the previous meticulous pace of the narrative. The ratio of narrative length to time within the plot changes abruptly as the courtship narrated over hundreds of pages leads to a marriage recounted with a handful of words. Each of Austen's novels ends with a marriage that has, almost until the last moment, seemed beyond the characters' abilities to arrange, and then, with the ultimate convention of fiction—drawing to a close—Austen undermines the supposed perfection of the sudden alliance by her equally sudden silence.

Some of Austen's readers have been disturbed by what they see as the contrived and truncated endings of her novels. As one recent biographer, John Halperin, has written, "If she has one overriding fault as a writer, it is her obvious and over-hasty desire, near the ends of her novels, to . . . get the thing over with" (1984: 78). Following Marvin Mudrick (1952), Halperin interprets this fault psychologically, attributing Austen's ironic sensibility to a capacity for moral "detachment," even "coldness," that allowed her both to assess the foibles of others and to protect herself from her own strongest passions (1984: 36–37). According to Halperin, the "distress" of Austen's characters "interests her more than their happiness," hence the over-hasty endings that allowed her to avoid feelings too painful to be expressed: "she cannot bring herself to write a final love scene" (78, 250).

Mary Poovey also faults Austen's endings. For the most part, argues Poovey, Austen wrote realistically about the ideological contradictions that women faced as modesty and propriety required them to assert their attractiveness negatively, by denying sexuality and self-assertion (1984: 23–28). Yet Austen's endings, Poovey claims, represent a turning away from "social realism and criticism" and an "escape into romance" (206), since they suggest to Poovey that Austen intended her readers to believe that private, individual choice might lead to gender justice—the reform of the patriarchal order by the perfect marriages of the heroines. For Poovey, "those fairy-tale marriages" of Austen's endings "stop realism dead in its tracks" (1984: 238; cf. Duckworth 1971).

Neither Halperin's nor Poovey's argument considers the possibility that the 'failure' of Austen's endings is something intentional. In our view, these endings instantiate a final comment on the provisional—indeed, fictional—status of any and all human judgments, even those of the heroines, and any and all accounts of social realities, even those of the narrators. To illustrate our point, we consider again *Mansfield Park*, which is difficult for the contemporary reader not only for the drama of *Lover's Vows* but for the problematic marriage that brings the novel to a close. Fanny Price's marriage to her cousin Edmund Bertram is first mentioned only three pages before the last of the novel's 473 pages, following the dramatic collapse of the possible alliances between Edmund and Mary Crawford and between Fanny and Mary's brother, Henry: "Scarcely had [Edmund] done regretting Mary Crawford, and observing to Fanny how impossible it was that he should ever meet with such another woman, before it began to strike him . . . whether Fanny herself were not growing as dear, as important to him . . . as Mary Crawford had ever been" (*MP* 470). The very next paragraph insists on the abruptness of this transformation:

I purposely abstain from dates on this occasion, that every one may be at liberty to fix their own, aware that the cure of unconquerable passions, and the transfer of unchanging attachments, must vary much as to time in different people.—I only intreat every body to believe that exactly at the time when it was quite natural that it should be so, and not a week earlier, Edmund did cease to care about Miss Crawford, and became as anxious to marry Fanny, as Fanny herself could desire. (*MP* 470)

Thus the change of attachments exists outside the novel's normal passage of time and outside the expected course of events. The sudden appearance of the narrative voicing as a personified agent with incomplete knowledge (represented by the subject pronoun *I*) calls attention to this rupture in the fixity and predictability of human events. The plot takes a sudden turn at the end of *Mansfield Park*, and the narration simultaneously exposes the fiction of narrative authority.[4]

Mansfield Park is, however, more complicated than this analysis implies, for if readers reread or remember the novel, they discover that the possibility of Fanny marrying one of her cousins was mentioned at the outset. The novel opens with the elders of the Bertram family debating the adoption of an impoverished niece, a passage discussed previously in chapter 3. Sir Thomas fears that Fanny, who would bring neither dowry nor rank to her marriage, will marry one of his sons, thus costing the Bertram estate the opportunity of making a valuable alliance. Mrs. Norris argues that because it is "morally impossible," incest can be preempted if the cousins are brought up as siblings (*MP* 6). *Mansfield Park* thus opens with a discussion of how to prevent a marriage that remains unmentioned until the final chapter. But in the final chapter this marriage turns out not only to be possible but—even in the eyes of Sir Thomas—desirable, how-

4. D. A. Miller (1981) is alert to much of the absence of authoritative closure in Austen's narratives; yet, like the critics we have discussed above, Miller takes Austen's endings as unironic reports of the completion of the protagonists' tales: "Jane Austen's fiction . . . is rigorously designed in terms of a resolution that leaves no residue or excess meaning to be told . . ." (19).

ever much it replaces marriages that would have provided both Fanny and Edmund with considerably greater wealth. Furthermore, while Mrs. Norris has wrongly predicted that Fanny "will never be more to either than a sister" (*MP* 7), she has not been entirely wrong, for, as we saw in chapter 5, until Fanny replaces Mary Crawford as the object of Edmund's romantic affections, Edmund consistently thinks of Fanny as a sister. His fraternal stance is evident even when he first considers marrying Fanny: "it began to strike him . . . whether it might not be a possible, an hopeful undertaking to persuade her that her warm and sisterly regard for him would be foundation enough for wedded love" (*MP* 470).

The marriage of Fanny and Edmund inverts the expected course of events in at least three ways: (1) it is incestlike, (2) it replaces matches of greater utilitarian value, and (3) it preempts a system of interrelated marriages that could have ended the novel with matches for all the young people at Mansfield Park. Two of Austen's previous novels (*Sense and Sensibility* and *Pride and Prejudice*) end with just such a system of interrelated matches, and a similar ending is set up as a possibility for *Mansfield Park*, with Mary and Henry Crawford marrying the cousins Edmund and Fanny. However, these inversions do not render the plot inchoate and incoherent. For in retrospect, even the least expected aspects of the novel become intelligible, or, more exactly, gain an alternative intelligibility. For instance, by coyly refusing to narrate the timing of the change in Edmund's romantic affections, the narrator indirectly raises the question of the extent to which Fanny and Edmund's relationship had previously involved (latent) romantic feelings. On the one hand, until the novel's abrupt ending, nothing in their behavior toward one another conforms to the standard pattern of flirtation and romance. As we saw in chapter 5, in the eyes of their watchful family and friends, Fanny and Edmund always seem like siblings. On the other hand, Fanny, normally quiet and reserved, reflects on her jealousy of Mary Crawford with atypical passion: "It was her intention . . . to try to overcome . . . all that bordered on selfishness in her affection for Edmund. . . . To think of him as Mary Crawford might be justified in thinking, would in her be insanity" (*MP* 264). In retrospect, the reader can see this unusual passage as foreshadowing the outcome of the novel, and Fanny might look back at it with secret delight. But these are reinterpretations, for in its presence it is, for Fanny, "insanity."

A careful examination of *Mansfield Park* reveals that Fanny's and Edmund's feelings for each other are neither romantic nor siblinglike, but something of both. In finding romance in the coresidential childhood of cousins, Austen is not replacing a mistaken set of positive, determining social categories with another; rather, her argument is against the fixity of all such categories, and she devotes the greatest portion of the final chapter to reminding the reader that the novel could have turned out the other way (cf. Simpson [1870] 1968: 245; Tanner 1986: 172). Thus Austen reminds the ethnographically minded reader that any narration or understanding of social life must take into account a multiplicity of alternatives—even those that only might have been. Social life, at least in Jane Austen's view, is a multiplicity of stories—constructed from a variety of contrastive points of view—that must nonetheless be told together.

CHAPTER EIGHT

Dialogue and Translation

I n chapter 7 we examined aspects of Jane Austen's narrative technique that make her works exemplars of dialogic discourse. We found modes of writing (and reading) that generate new meanings and new understandings—that is, new language—through the process of describing the interaction and relations between multiple realities. We also suggested that the multiplicity of Austen's narratives might serve as an example to anthropologists who have generally assumed a more unitary and authoritative voice in texts self-consciously constructed to be nonfiction.

In this chapter we turn our attention more specifically to ethnographic writing, and in particular to the problem of translation between multiple realities that all ethnographic writing must confront. Following Stocking (1983b), we begin by noting that the history of anthropology contains two prominent strands that differ profoundly in their approaches to human diversity. On the one hand, anthropology is heir to a scientific tradition that has sought to discover and report the facts of that diversity. This project requires an objective and truth-preserving language that is itself independent of cultural values. With a commitment to the ideals of truth and enlightenment, some practitioners have attempted to build, and would have us continue, a science of humanity situated at an objective distance from culture; that is, a study of culture that is realistic and not itself a cultural product. There is, of course, an opposing tendency in anthropology's complex history, equally motivated, at least in its historical origin, by a faith in enlightenment (cf. Boon 1982: 27–49). A desire to show the unity of mankind has instigated an interpretive social science dedicated to finding, accepting, and celebrating the sense of seemingly irrational cultures. For this anthropology, the appearance of irrationality is an illusion created by cultural difference—a failure to understand alternative constructions of reality. Thus, whereas the first strand in anthropological history privileges a singular reality, the second posits a plurality of constructed realities.

The tension between them, though never resolved, is commonly dissipated by a comforting sleight of hand: anthropologists adopt the stance of reporting—realistically, of course—the constructed reality of others; we describe, and explain, what is real to them. This formula conveniently maintains both our commitment to the real and a sense of cultural difference, but it does so hierarchically. It is *our* realism that describes *their* realities: we practice and teach a science of their myths and not a myth-logic of our sciences. We translate their reality into our terms, thereby maintaining the authority of our language as the ultimate point of reference. This is convenient; our language is, after all, the language that we know. Yet if our language—our reality—is only one particularity amongst others, then surely anthropology must learn to see it as such. To do so requires not merely that we translate alternative realities into our own, but equally that we translate ours into . . . into what?

Here we run into difficulties, for translation, as usually conceived and practiced, presumes that one begins with an adequate language. By contrast, we seek the capacity to construct language that openly admits its inadequacies—that recognizes its need for alternatives. In brief, we seek a process of translation in which our initial language changes as it engages others, in which our language does not adopt a posture of merely describing what is real to those others, but questions its own reality while engaging the reality of others—and vice versa.

It is here that we turn to Jane Austen. What Austen's fiction offers ethnography is not the freedom to 'make it up' but an example of writing that enables dialogue between alternative, sometimes contradictory, voices and perspectives. Allowing such dialogue does not, however, mean that Austen's writing always, or even typically, resolves conflicts between divergent perspectives. Indeed, rather than providing some balanced view that mediates all disputes of fact and value, Austen's dialogic narration frequently demonstrates the impossibility of such resolution. As we have argued repeatedly in the preceding chapters, no single perspective within Austen's work—no single narration and no single reading—can encompass the multiplicity (and provisionality) of realities. In the present chapter we turn our attention to the portrayal of multiple realities in anthropological writing, examining one of the best-known anthropological translations of an alien reality: Evans-Pritchard's Zande magic. We go on to examine this example of Evans-Pritchard's ethnography in the light of Jane Austen's.

Authority over the Untrue:
Mangu, Soroka, *and* Ngua *at Oxbridge*

The Azande, reports Evans-Pritchard, believe in *mangu,* and, moreover, they frequently explain misfortune in terms of *mangu*:

> Shortly after my arrival in Zandeland we were passing through a government settlement and noticed that a hut had been burnt to the ground. . . . Its owner was overcome with grief since it had contained the beer he was preparing for a mortuary feast. He told us that he had gone the previous night to examine his beer. He had lit a handful of straw and raised it above his head so that light would be cast on the pots, and in so doing he had ignited the thatch. He, and my companions also, were convinced that the disaster was *caused* by MANGU. (1937: 66; Zande original added in small capital letters)

Evans-Pritchard translated *mangu* as "witchcraft." Thus: "he, and my companions also, were convinced that the disaster was *caused* by witchcraft" (66, witchcraft in translation).

In other words, the Azande believe in a type of causality that Westerners, particularly Western academics, reject as both false and irrational. Thus, in Zandeland, Evans-Pritchard confronts a classic problem of cross-cultural anthropology: How can the ethnographer comprehend and explain apparently irrational beliefs—specifically, Zande beliefs in *mangu, soroka,* and *ngua,* translated by Evans-Pritchard as "witchcraft," "oracles," and "magic"?

To return to the grieving hut owner, why would he, and other Azande, explain the fire in terms of witchcraft? After all, the Azande quite clearly had a practical knowledge of fire. The answer, says Evans-Pritchard, lies in the aspect of the event that is being explained. The Azande know quite well that "[it] is a universal quality of fire to burn," but "it is not a universal quality of fire to burn *you.* This may never happen; or once in a lifetime, and then only if you have been bewitched" (69). In sum: "It is the particular and variable conditions of an event and not the general and universal conditions that witchcraft [MANGU] explains" (69; Zande original added).

In his most famous illustration of the point, Evans-Pritchard narrates not an actual event but the hypothetical—some might say fictional—collapse of an old granary onto people seeking shade below: "In Zandeland sometimes an old granary collapses. . . . It may happen that there are people sitting beneath the granary when it collapses and they are injured, for it is a heavy structure made of beams and clay and may be stored with eleusine as well" (69).

Thus, unlike scientific notions of cause, *mangu* causality is not, to quote from the dictionary at hand, a "relationship between . . . regularly correlated events or phenomena," but some sort of propositional statement about particularities. By contrast, says Evans-Pritchard: "We [the implicit community of author and reader] have no explanation of why two chains of causation intersected at a certain time and place, *for there is no interdependence between them*" (70, emphasis added).

The Azande, then, are wrong; co-occurrence is just coincidence, without rhyme or reason, regardless of the misfortune experienced by human beings. And, of course, there aren't any witches:

It is an inevitable conclusion from Zande descriptions of witchcraft that it is not an objective reality. The physiological condi-

tion which is said to be the seat of witchcraft, and which I
believe to be nothing more than food passing through the small
intestine, is an objective condition, but the qualities they attribute to it and the rest of their beliefs about it are mystical.
Witches, as the Azande conceive them, cannot exist. (63)

Witchcraft is not real but only an "idiom" in which Azande "speak
about" misfortune (64). Moreover, witchcraft accusations are not, as
the Azande believe, divined from oracles but are expressions of social tensions amongst the Azande. In Evans-Pritchard's concise summary: "In a study of Zande MANGU we must bear in mind, firstly, that
the notion is a function of situations of misfortune, and, secondly,
that it is a function of personal relations" (106, Zande original
added).

There are, then, reasons behind the irrational belief in *mangu,* but
unlike Evans-Pritchard, the Azande misunderstand those reasons
and misconstrue their own idiom for discussing misfortune and personal relations as witchcraft. Evans-Pritchard argues not simply that
the Azande are comprehensible but, more specifically, that he can do
the comprehending—and then share it with his readers. Throughout *Witchcraft, Oracles, and Magic* Evans-Pritchard maintains a distance between the discourse of his book, shared by author and
reader, and the Azande, the object observed and analyzed by that
discourse. To cite a simple example, in his preface Evans-Pritchard
concludes an expression of gratitude to the Azande by noting that he
inscribes his thanks "even though the Azande will never see them in
print" (viii). More complexly, a few pages later the reader finds a
tripartite typology of "mystical," "common-sense" and "scientific"
thought, arranged typographically as three distinct entries in a glossary. In this table of technical terms, Evans-Pritchard writes: "Mystical notions . . . attribute to phenomena supra-sensible qualities
which . . . they do not possess." By contrast, common sense is
based on "what can logically be inferred from observation," that is,
on "experience and rules of thumb." Finally, even more unlike mystical notions, science depends on "experiment and rules of Logic,"
and whereas "common sense observes only some links in a chain of
causation, . . . science observes all" (12). Moreover, Zande knowl-

edge of science is "meagre" if not nonexistent, and Western science must thus be used as "the sole arbiter" of which Zande notions are mystical and which are commonsensical (64, 12). In sum, Evans-Pritchard's glossary not only maintains the distance between Zande and Western modes of knowing reality, it arranges them hierarchically as well.

It is worth noting that in a discussion of his fieldwork experience, Evans-Pritchard describes himself as having abandoned such distance when he lived and worked among the Azande:

> In my own culture . . . I rejected, and reject, Zande notions of witchcraft. In their culture, in the set of ideas I then lived in, I accepted them; in a kind of way I believed them. Azande were talking about witchcraft daily, both among themselves and to me; any communication was well-nigh impossible unless one took witchcraft for granted. You cannot have a remunerative, even intelligent, conversation with people about something they take as self-evident if you give them the impression that you regard their belief as an illusion or a delusion. Mutual understanding, and with it sympathy, would soon be ended. . . . Anyhow, I had to act as though I trusted the Zande oracles and therefore to give assent to their dogmas of witchcraft, whatever reservations I might have. If I wanted to go hunting or on a journey, for instance, no one would willingly accompany me unless I was able to produce a verdict of the poison oracle that all would be well, that witchcraft did not threaten our project; and if one goes on arranging one's affairs, organizing one's life in harmony with the lives of one's hosts, whose companionship one seeks and without which one would sink into disorientated craziness, one must eventually give way, or at any rate partially give way. If one must act as though one believed, one ends in believing, or half-believing as one acts. (1976: 244)

Here Evans-Pritchard gives a compelling account of how the ethnographer enters an alternative cultural idiom and comes to experience the world in its terms. By contrast, presenting his scientific analysis of the other's culture, Evans-Pritchard describes his own participation in the witchcraft idiom as nothing other than a "lapse into unreason" (1937: 99). Taken together, the two texts suggest that the ethnographer can act in accord with native believers, but such participation remains a fieldwork technique, a self-conscious exercise in irrationality.

But why do Azande rely on beliefs that we know to be erroneous? This is particularly vexing because Evans-Pritchard reports that the Azande are "sophisticated and progressive" (13) and possess technical knowledge: "They have a sound working knowledge of nature in so far as it concerns their welfare" (80). How is it possible, then, that they so consistently delude themselves when it comes to *mangu*? The answer to this question, implicit throughout Evans-Pritchard's account, lies in the homogeneity of Zande culture, the seamlessness of their traditions, and their concomitant lack of reflexive awareness. In Evans-Pritchard's view, the Azande are all alike: "Since [Zande] behavior is fixed by tradition it is mainly alike in every instance, and one has only to describe the customary procedure" (99). Similarly, statements about the fixity of Zande traditions occur throughout Evans-Pritchard's text: "Witch doctors," he writes, "have *always* been a part of Zande culture" (194, emphasis added). Zande culture and society is, in sum, undifferentiated and homogeneous, free of either synchronic or diachronic variation, and hence free of intra-cultural dialogue, difference, and dispute. For Evans-Pritchard, the Azande are an object amenable to analysis, not subjects involved in analysis of their own. Thus the Azande can be portrayed through the construction—some might say fiction—of a generic Zande:

> Within the environmental and cultural limits which I have sketched lives the Zande, hoeing his gardens, hunting, paying his visits to court, pursuing litigation, quarrelling with his neighbours, dancing, and fulfilling each day his obligations as subject, father, husband, son, brother, and so on. As we watch him carrying out the many economic and social tasks of day-to-day existence we are amazed at the extensive part of his life which is given over to oracles and magic and other ritual performances. (19)

Recurring representations of such generic Zande activities prepares the reader to accept Evans-Pritchard's claim that the Azande are given to feeling, reaction, and mystical notions, but not to scientific analysis (80, 82, 99). From Evans-Pritchard's account, one would think that it is only the presence of Europeans that rouses the Azande to reflection: "it is we who question them about their beliefs and by our innovations challenge them; they enact them and feel little urge to explain them" (82). Unfortunately, the Zande response to such enlightened prompting is "determined intellectual resistance" rather than the development of a scientific spirit (1936: 291). "Their idiom," he tells us, "is so much of a mystical order that criticism of one belief can only be made in terms of another that equally lacks foundation in fact" (1937: 194).

As evidence for this view Evans-Pritchard attempts to demonstrate that Zande thought contains "contradictions" that author and reader can perceive but which elude the Azande. For example, Azande associate witchcraft with a physical substance lodged somewhere in the belly. This "witchcraft-substance" is, moreover, an inherited material, passing from a man to his sons and from a woman to her daughters. Evans-Pritchard argues that "to our minds it appears evident that if a man is proven a witch [all the males of] his clan are *ipso facto* witches, since the Zande clan is a group of persons related biologically . . . through the male line."[1] Azande, he goes on, understand but do not accept this argument, for "it would involve

---

1. Where we have inserted material within brackets, Evans-Pritchard's original reads: "if a man is proven a witch *the whole* of his clan are ipso facto witches" (restored material in italics). Taken literally, then, Evans-Pritchard's text tells us that if a man is a witch, then both the males and the females of a clan are witches. This appears to contradict Evans-Pritchard's report that witchcraft is inherited from a same-sex parent, for if a man's witchcraft substance is inherited only by his sons, and not his daughters, there is no reason why "the whole of his clan," including the females, should be witches. This seeming contradiction in a proof of the illogicality of others has given us more than a few moments of pause. Pending a more persuasive interpretation, we have posited that by "the whole of his clan" Evans-Pritchard meant only the males of the clan. This may not be logical, but it undoubtedly fits Evans-Pritchard's own cultural "idiom." In interpreting this puzzle it is important to note that Evans-Pritchard is consistent in his reports of the rules of inheritance for clan membership and witchcraft (Evans-Pritchard 1932, 1933, and 1936).

the whole notion of witchcraft in contradiction were they to do so." In Evans-Pritchard's view, "Azande do not perceive the contradiction as we perceive it because they have no theoretical interest in the subject" (24-25).

Yet, despite this claim, Evans-Pritchard presents abundant evidence to suggest that Azande have great theoretical interest in witchcraft and, indeed, possess an elaborate theory of what it means to be a witch. It seems that witchcraft substance may remain "cool" (that is, inactive) in a person's stomach, so a person may have witchcraft substance within him or her during an entire lifetime without ever being a witch (25). Thus, being a witch is not, for the Azande, a fixed and permanent characteristic of persons but a situational component of relations. "A person who has bewitched a man is not viewed by him ever afterwards as a witch but only at the time of the misfortune he has caused and in relation to these special conditions" (107). If it is not the physical witchcraft substance that makes people be witches, then there is no contradiction between the Zande account of the inheritance of witchcraft substance and their claim that one man in a clan can be a witch and not others.

Evans-Pritchard, however, fails to consider such alternative interpretations, maintaining resolutely that scientific logic can demonstrate contradictions in Zande thought. In this cross-cultural analysis the language of analysis supersedes its constituted object. Evans-Pritchard, not the Azande, reduces witchcraft to an essential material substance. Evans-Pritchard, not the Azande, employs a reified conception of a person. In sum, Evans-Pritchard's authoritative voice replaces, rather than engages, Zande voices. (A summary of Evans-Pritchard's proof of Zande illogic and our proposed alternative interpretation is shown in Figure 1.)

As a second illustration of the relation of Evans-Pritchard's text to Zande reasoning, consider again that often-read, often-taught, and often-cited discussion of the granary. Let us recall that the collapse of the granary is a hypothetical example, presented as an inductive conclusion to a series of Zande witchcraft events narrated by Evans-Pritchard. Thus, with the granary example *Witchcraft, Oracles, and Magic* shifts gears, moving from a reportage of "unfortunate events" which Azande have themselves attributed to "witchcraft" to Evans-

FIGURE I.

Evans-Pritchard's Proof: A Contradiction in Zande Thought
1. Azande claim witchcraft substance is inherited from same-sex parent.
2. The Azande clan is a group of persons related through the male line.
3. "If a man is proven a witch [all the males] of his clan are *ipso facto* witches."
4. Azande often claim that one member of a clan is a witch and not others.
5. Propositions 3 and 4 are logical opposites. *Therefore Zande thought allows contradictions.*

Alternative Interpretation
1. Witchcraft substance is inherited, but it is not this physical substance that makes one a witch.
2. Rather, *being* a witch is a situational feature of social relations.
3. Hence, one man in a clan can *be* a witch and not others.
4. *Thus, in this example, there is no evidence of contradiction in Zande thought.*

Pritchard's analysis of those attributions. Whereas the granary's collapse is represented as a generic event ("in Zandeland sometimes an old granary collapses"), the previous examples are narrated as particular cases, providing evidence of "the Zande's explicit line of reasoning—not my own" (68):

> A boy knocked his foot against a small stump of wood in the center of a bush path . . . and suffered pain and inconvenience in consequence. . . . He declared that witchcraft had made him knock his foot against the stump. . . . I told the boy that he had knocked his foot against the stump of wood because he had been careless, and that witchcraft had not placed it in the path, for it had grown there naturally. He agreed that witchcraft had

nothing to do with the stump being in his path but added that he had kept his eyes open for stumps, as indeed every Zande does most carefully, and that if he had not been bewitched he would have seen the stump. As a conclusive argument for his view he remarked that all cuts do not take days to heal but, on the contrary, close quickly, for that is the nature of cuts. Why, then, had his sore festered and remained open, if there was no witchcraft behind it? (65–66)

In this and other dialogic examples, it emerges, in every case, that the Azande employ the term *mangu* to explain circumstances in which human beings—their senses, judgment, and bodily functions—fail, and in failing cause misfortune. Only in the granary example does the "misfortune" attributed to witchcraft involve pure coincidence without a failing of human capacities. If this reading is correct, then rather than capturing the general features of the previous cases, Evans-Pritchard's most famous illustration overpowers the Zande voices of his own ethnography and replaces their explicit reasoning with his own.

Finally, let us return to the central problematic of Evans-Pritchard's text: the translation of *mangu, soroka,* and *ngua* as "witchcraft," "oracles," and "magic." Early in the book Evans-Pritchard states that his goal in translating has been "to make a number of English words stand for Zande notions" by consistently using "the same [English] term only and always when the same [Zande] notion is being discussed." He adds that this consistency guarantees a faithful translation because "terms are only labels which help us to sort out facts of the same kind from facts which are different." Briefly put, in Evans-Pritchard's account of translation, words are mere signifiers, or labels, for preexisting categories, and are not signifieds constituting the categories of our thought. Yet Evans-Pritchard's complex text belies such a simplistic mode of translation. For instance, he writes: "To say that witchcraft has blighted the groundnut crop . . . is equivalent to saying in our own culture that the groundnut crop has failed owing to blight. . . . Witchcraft is a classification of misfortunes which while differing from each other in other respects have this single common character: their harmfulness to man" (64). And elsewhere: "The Zande phrase 'it is witchcraft' may often be translated simply as 'it is bad'" (107).

Let us insist, however, that it is not "witchcraft" that can be translated "bad" but *"mangu."* By implication, then, "it is *mangu*" may often be translated as "it is bad." Yet, if this is true, then what justifies the invariant translation of *mangu* by the English term *witchcraft* rather than *bad*? After all, some of us sometimes speak of bad luck and only mean misfortune. Did Zande use of the term *mangu* always entail as literal a belief in witches as Evans-Pritchard's translation suggests? Was it only Evans-Pritchard who recognized that *mangu* provided an idiom for speaking of misfortune and social tensions? If turnabout were not just fair play but a historical possibility, a Zande ethnographer might explain discussions of stampeding bulls and hibernating bears with a complementary formula: "animistic beliefs provide the British—and the Americans—an idiom with which to speak of their mystified financial markets" (cf. Taussig 1980: 31; Keesing 1985).

Our point is not to deny that *mangu* involved mystical notions, but to suggest that Evans-Pritchard's use of the word *witchcraft* in translation is not sufficiently flexible to deal with the nuances of Zande thought and communication. Similarly, Evans-Pritchard's translation is closed to nonreified conceptions of the person and to Zande insights into the causal consequences of social tensions. In sum, Evans-Pritchard attributes to the Zande belief in *mangu* a simpleminded literalness, but that literalness is found in translation.

Dialogic Translation and Defamiliarization

Writing about a world she had experienced from birth, Jane Austen did not face the problem of radical translation that Evans-Pritchard confronted. Nonetheless, she did not write unreflexively about a taken-for-granted world; rather, she disintegrated its homogeneity, representing the interrelations among multiple voices without privileging any one of them with unassailable authority. In Austen's narrations, the alter-cultural transgression of cultural rules sets those rules into dialogic relief, and thus allows foreigners like ourselves an entrance to a social reality other than our own. Austen thus provides a more general model for communicating (and interpreting) meaning across social difference—a problem of which cross-cultural translation is merely an extreme case. In finding degrees of translation in all exchanges of meaning—in all acts of communication—we follow Jakobson, himself following Peirce:

> As linguists and as ordinary word-users, the meaning of any linguistic sign is its translation into some further, alternative sign, especially a sign "in which it is more fully developed," as Peirce . . . insistently stated. . . . We distinguish three ways of interpreting a verbal sign: it may be translated into other signs of the same language, into another language, or into another, nonverbal system of symbols. (Jakobson 1959: 233)

As an example of Austen's dialogic translations within a language, consider again her handling of incest in *Mansfield Park.* By painstakingly developing a story that results in a marriage between persons brought up like brother and sister, Austen allows us to perceive the incest taboo as a social rule; that is, as a principle of meaning open to negotiation and negation. More specifically, the tale of *Mansfield Park* succeeds in making Fanny and Edmund marital choices for each other, notwithstanding both their coresidential childhood and their ties of blood. It thus emphatically marks marital choice as what incest (normally) is not. In other words, *Mansfield Park* illuminates the cultural meanings of incest and marriage by an explicit transformation of the former into the latter. We learn what each term means (in part) from a tale that treats them both as units of (transformable) meaning.

In complementary fashion, in reading Jane Austen, or any other culture, we would employ a category like incest not to ask the inevitable universalistic question but provisionally, as a means of probing how various people understand, and transgress, endogamous limits. In so doing we would expect to find limits previously unimagined, and thus new meanings for our points of departure—'incest' and 'marriage.' We would expect that in each interpretation of meaning across cultures, our initial term would be displaced by the difference—the realities—of others (cf. Boon and Schneider 1974). Our point is this: reality—provisional, interpretive, and pluralistic—is best served not by realism but by the engagement of difference; that is, by dialogic narration, reading, and translation. Despite its claims to authority, realism is not, dare we say it, realistic; it objectifies in observation and misconstrues in translation and narration. We thus propose a dialogic alternative not simply for ethnography but also for the analysis and translation of meaning across cultures. Dialogue, in this formulation, refers not to a happy conversation between two parties, but to a process that allows voices of ever greater disparity and contradiction to speak together without any one voice or any one language overpowering the others.[2] Such dialogue would not lead to the discovery of some unified or universal language that can encompass all languages. Rather, it would allow our interactions with the realities of others to displace our native categories, thereby pluralizing our language. In place of some universal system of translation that would map the signifiers of one language on to the signifieds of another—that would allow one language to be replaced by another—we seek instead heteroglossia.

2. For critiques of the romanticization of dialogue in anthropology, see Handler (1985) and Buckley (1987).

CHAPTER NINE

But What, Then, of Reality?

There is one precept of British anthropology—perhaps the only one in the name of which I can call myself an ethnographer—by which the native is always right, if he leads the investigator in an unexpected direction. If the ethnographer is led astray, . . . if his hypotheses collapse one after the other in contact with native reality even though he sets up his investigation with great care, these are signs that we are dealing with an empirical science and not science fiction.—Jeanne Favret-Saada (1980: 13)

I am a realist writer because I believe that in Latin America everything is possible, everything is real. There is a technical problem in that the writer finds difficulty in transcribing real events in Latin America because no one would believe them in a book.—Gabriel García Márquez (quoted by Wilson Harris [1970: 24])

I n the earlier chapters of this book we approached Jane Austen's novels as though they contained the record of a social world amenable to cultural analysis of the kind typically practiced by symbolic anthropologists. Indeed, as we worked we at times carried on as though we had entered a social world and were practicing field research within it. In the last three chapters our focus has shifted from the world Austen created to the narrative and interpretive techniques used to create it. Chapter 6 examined the interpretive skills of various characters within the social world of the novels; chapter 7 analyzed some of the narrative techniques that Austen used to create the novels themselves; and chapter 8 applied some of the lessons learned from Austen to the problem of ethnographic translation. But the doubled focus of our analysis generates a peculiar tension, for how can we treat Austen's texts as both data and analysis? The question is likely to be particularly troubling for social scientists for whom fictional texts have typically been suspect both as sources of data and as models of analysis.

Though positivist notions of fact and fiction make one wary of using novels in either capacity, recent scholarship in a number of disciplines such as history, literary theory, and anthropology has focused attention on the fictional qualities of all texts, including those that employ rhetorical styles marking themselves as objective.[1] For the most part, the attack on the distinction between fact and fiction has brought forth a multitude of concerns about the limits of knowledge in the human sciences. Deprived of confidence in the factualness of the accounts produced by social research, many have wondered what, if any, basis remains for a science of human societies, cultures, and histories.

In this concluding chapter we seek a more positive result from the critique of scientific realism. Specifically, we seek the strengths of literary narrative qua literary narrative for social analysis; in particular, we seek the ability of Jane Austen's complex, multivocal narratives to help us understand a social world that is partially foreign and partially familiar by setting its organizing principles into dialogic relief. In so doing we locate Austen's texts as a form of social action which communicates with and about its constitutive principles of meaning. Our aim is thus not to evade the question of the

1. From among a burgeoning literature challenging commonsense notions of the divide between ethnography and literature, works that have been particularly useful to us include Errington (1979), Boon (1982), Marcus and Fischer (1986), and Clifford (1988).

texts' representation of reality, but to replace it with a more complex formulation that presumes neither the distinctness of fiction and fact—the world of the texts and the world of the world—nor the distinctness of data and analysis.

This chapter discusses the relationship of the Austen texts to the real world. In an attempt to redefine realism, we leave behind notions of mimesis and accuracy to consider the capacity of dialogic modes of narration, like those practiced by Jane Austen, to communicate cultural realities across cultural differences. We begin by relating Austen's fictional narratives to some nonfictional writings relevant to our present concerns: polemical social analyses written by two of Austen's contemporaries: Edmund Burke and Mary Wollstonecraft. Following this comparison, we examine Austen's *Juvenilia* in relation to shifts in the meaning and valuation of realism in eighteenth- and nineteenth-century literary criticism. We use this discussion to reexamine the separation of science and literature as genres and modes of knowing the world.

Burke, Wollstonecraft, and Austen

Recent critical discussions of Jane Austen have tended increasingly to focus on the irony and ambiguity of her work while rejecting older images of Austen as the last proponent of eighteenth-century moral order (see, for example, the work of Cottom [1985] and Poovey [1984]). A particularly interesting example of this perspective is an essay by L. J. Swingle, who relates Austen's narrative strategies to an enlarging European consciousness of moral diversity during her time. According to Swingle, the increased awareness of moral diversity had been expressed in romantic writers' concern for questions of 'party.' Commenting on Blake's reading of *Paradise Lost* ("Blake claims that Milton was 'of the Devil's party without knowing it'"), Swingle observes that what had been a distinction between Truth and Error for Milton was for Blake a distinction of party; that is, a distinction resulting from "different systems of thought or shared assumptions concerning the true and the false" (1979: 220–21). Swingle argues that the awareness of multiple 'cultures' (to impose the twentieth-century term) produced a kind of hypercorrection in political argumentation: "We hold these truths to be self-evident—but this suggests that someone else out there is busy holding other truths equally self-evident" (221; cf. Poovey 1984: 180). Swingle then contrasts Austen's work to such polemical writing, developing an interpretation similar to the position taken throughout the present book: "One of Jane Austen's primary literary preoccupations is with confrontation and interaction among characters who feel differently, but who do not . . . recognize that they are operating within contrary systems of thought" (225).

Summing up these insights, we might say that Austen interrelates viewpoints conventionally separated in other narrative genres. To illustrate this point we will compare Austen's writing about a central, yet contested, aspect of her world to some exemplary non-fictional writings on the same topic. As we have seen (chapter 4), the Austen novels explore an issue that was, and remains, central to Western political discourse: the relationship between merit and rank. This issue—in the form of debates about the rights of man versus the rights of property—was crucial to political philosophers from before the Revolution of 1688 to the Reform Bill of 1832 and beyond. If we turn to tracts on these issues published in England during Jane Austen's lifetime, we often find polemical accounts in which one perspective is granted a monopoly on rationality and truth, and alternatives are presented via caricatures and stereotypes that do little to explore their alternative rationality; for such exploration would, of course, belie the claim that truth and rationality belong solely to one party.

In comparing such essays in political argument to Austen's fiction, we pose this question: Can these texts equal Austen's in teaching us the distinctions of another world of meaning? If, for example, we look at Burke's *Reflections on the Revolution in France*, we find the rights of property vociferously defended in a rhetoric that appeals constantly to the natural order of the universe. For Burke, "the characteristic essence of property . . . is to be *unequal*," and, moreover, "great masses" of property, duly protected by the laws of civil society, "form a natural rampart about lesser properties in their gradations." Thus the English landed estate "tends . . . to the perpetuation of society itself"; and "the possessors of family wealth, and of the distinction which attends hereditary possession . . . are the natural securities for this transmission" ([1790] 1968: 140–41; emphasis in original). Further, though the social contract grants all citizens the right to enjoy their property unmolested, those who control more property ought to have more choice—a greater "share of power, authority, and direction . . . in the management of the state" (150). Burke finds the desire to preserve property and rank "implanted in our nature" (245), and he appeals to the ancients in his argument that the different "descriptions" (291) of men in society are "as . . . so many different species of animals" (299). Thus hierarchy within society follows inevitably from natural law, and those who would level distinctions "only change and pervert the natural order" (138).

In opposition to Burke, Mary Wollstonecraft mocks "English liberty" as nothing other than "security of property" ([1790] 1960: 24). She consistently argues that independence ought to stem from reason rather than property ([1790] 1960: 92; [1792] 1967: 52), and that women, like all humans, irrespective of their rank in existing society, owe their "first duty . . . to themselves as rational creatures" ([1792] 1967: 218). For Wollstonecraft, "the perpetuation of property in our families" actually corrupts natural familial bonds. Parents tyrannize children in order to aggrandize the family estate, forcing them into marriages that violate their "natural" inclinations. Similarly, the practice of primogeniture to keep estates intact leads to countless "unnatural crimes": "The younger children have been sacrificed to the eldest son; sent into exile, or confined in convents, that they might not encroach on what was called, with shameful falsehood, the *family* estate." By contrast, "natural parental affection . . . makes no difference between child and child, but what reason justifies by pointing out superior merit" ([1790] 1960: 44–46; emphasis in original).

Thus Wollstonecraft and Burke each assert that their view alone captures the "natural" basis for hierarchy: for Burke, nature sides with ancestral inheritance; for Wollstonecraft, with individual merit. Neither can see his or her position as relative, and both derisively caricature the opposite point of view. Note, for instance, how

Wollstonecraft uses images of primitivism ("younger children sacrificed") and, specifically, of primitive papistry ("sent [to] . . . convents") to sway her contemporary audience of "civilized" English Protestants.

In their consideration of rank, the Austen texts encompass the arguments of both Burke and Wollstonecraft, setting these voices (and others) in narratives that question the absoluteness (the naturalness) of the positions inscribed. We have already discussed how Austen's texts join Wollstonecraft in questioning the natural basis of aristocratic privilege. Her narratives similarly question the privileges both of eldest sons vis-à-vis their brothers and of men vis-à-vis women. For example, Tom Bertram, an eldest son of a wealthy and prominent family, is represented as inferior to his younger brother in merit, and Edward Ferrars is superior to his foppish brother, Robert, the principal heir to the family estate. In the Ferrars's case the irony is doubled. Edward is chronologically the elder brother, but his refusal to break an engagement with a social subordinate in order to marry the woman of his mother's choice (who would be an "advantageous match" for the family) causes his mother to legally reorder the birth order of the two brothers (*SS* 269). Here the relationship between an elder and younger brother, generally considered to be "naturally" immutable, is purposefully altered by a woman ostentatiously devoted to a rigid interpretation of hierarchy. Nature, in this particular case, conforms to the cultural ideal but is nonetheless altered, thereby exposing the conceit of the belief in society's foundation in nature. Finally, in Austen's novels women are as frequently shown to be superior to men as men are to women. When the lowly ranked Miss Fairfax is discovered to be engaged to Frank Churchill, who is as much her superior in rank as in fortune, even someone as punctilious with respect to rank as Emma can offer the following evaluation: "It is fit that the fortune should be on his side, for I think the merit will be all on hers" (*E* 420).

Although Austen consistently questions the naturalness of social inequalities, she does not replace this Burkean position with a belief in presocial, individual merit based in "nature." Indeed, here her texts leave Wollstonecraft and join Burke, recognizing the folly of ignoring established social conditions—though, unlike Burke, she denies the naturalness of the received social order. Let us briefly recall the social and personal problem that commonly serves as the focus for each novel: the selection of a spouse. As we have argued, Austen raises doubts both about decisions made only in terms of social hierarchy (good matches) and about those made solely in terms of personal merit (romance). In Austen's novels either criterion alone fails, both as a means of interpreting the suitability of a potential partner and as a means of building an increasingly close relationship between persons. Characters such as Marianne Dashwood advocate individualistic romance regardless of the social circumstances of the match, thereby simplistically denying the harsh realities of poverty; and characters such as Charlotte Lucas advocate marrying for social advantage, thereby forgoing the possibility of deep, mutual understanding and respect. In marriage, as elsewhere in social life, Austen suggests neither that the social facts of status be ignored nor that they be accepted without question.

In sum, the positions that occur in political writings as absolute (and mutually exclusive) truths occur in Austen as alternatives that are allowed to speak to, and about, each other. The polemic writings of Burke and Wollstonecraft proceed by unraveling points of view that are intertwined in social life. This forging of monologic voices notwithstanding, such writings are designated nonfiction. By contrast, Austen's fictions weave together diverse perspectives, thereby exploring the (often conflicting) cultural principles that structure the negotiation of social life. Thus Austen's novels transcend their reputation as tales of domestic life. Indeed, freed from the limitations of that unfortunate designation, her texts can provide an interpretive guide both to the political debates of her contemporaries and to the social realities her contemporaries debated.

Austen's Juvenilia *and Standards of Realism*

Our comparison of Austen with Burke and Wollstonecraft has brought us to question the received valuation of nonfiction and fiction as historical records. In chapter 8, a rereading of Evans-

Pritchard in the light of Austen's narrative techniques led us to reconsider the notion of translation generally presupposed in ethnological writing. We proceed now to a similar reexamination of the notion of *realism* as that term has been used to refer to the relationship between the real world and various textual genres. We approach this problem by examining Austen's *Juvenilia* in relation to changing eighteenth-century standards of novelistic excellence. During Austen's lifetime, older conceptions of the moral utility of fiction were being replaced by a notion of realism defined in terms of the detachment of observation and writing from the world being described and analyzed. We argue that an epistemology and aesthetic based on such realism constrain readings of the *Juvenilia* by confining them to a world of childish (hence unrealistic) imagination devoid of the possibility of serious alter-cultural critique.

Jane Austen's *Juvenilia* were written between 1787, when the author was twelve, and 1793. For the most part they are prose narratives, ranging in length from several paragraphs to several pages. There are also plays and epistolary novels. These writings are set in villages with names like Crankhumdunberry and Pammydiddle as well as in Berkshire, London, and Bath. In them, a mother abandons her infant, then, rediscovering her, adopts her as a foundling; a young woman falls in love with a hat; and a suitor wins his beloved's hand by murdering the man she prefers, though in the end he marries the dead man's sister to compensate her for the loss of her brother. With such incidents, it is not surprising that modern critics read the *Juvenilia* as a precociously brilliant satire of sentimental fiction coupled with a childish disregard of reality. As Brian Southam puts it:

> The earliest pieces display an intriguing mixture of elements. On the one hand, there is the naturally high-spirited fun of childhood, knockabout farce, fanciful extravagance, solemn nonsense, and elaborate wordplay. Yet there is also sophisticated humor, a knowing and knowledgeable pinpointing of the false values and absurd conventions of sentimental fiction. . .´. Then there are the weaknesses of rank bad writing—clumsy plots, action beyond the bounds of probability . . . and every variety of inconsequence and digression. (1986b: 246)

This description sanctions fanciful extravagance by explaining it as appropriate to childhood while condemning action beyond the bounds of probability. The realism appropriate to good novels, then, must avoid both childish fancy and improbability. But ought we so easily to dismiss fancy, childish or otherwise, and what are the moral and epistemological virtues of a realism devoid of it?

To answer these questions we need to situate Jane Austen's *Juvenilia* in relationship to the critical discourse of her time. The critique of sentimental fiction elaborated by the young Jane Austen and others represented, as A. Walton Litz points out, "a serious moral position" (1965: 6). Eighteenth-century criticism presumed that fiction could have an important influence on the reading public. Sentimental novels were condemned not merely because they were deemed unrealistic, but because they were thought to encourage readers, especially women, to indulge in the sentimental excesses of fictional heroines. For eighteenth-century critics, mimesis and moral effect were inseparable as criteria for judging the excellence of fiction. Yet during Jane Austen's lifetime those standards were changing. As M. H. Abrams has written, aesthetic theory in the Romantic era elevated science to an epistemologically decisive position as the opposite of poetry:

> It had been common since antiquity to oppose poetry to history, and to base this distinction on the ground that poetry imitates some form of the universal or ideal instead of the actual event. The usual procedure of romantic critics was to substitute science for history as the opposite of poetry, and to ground the distinction on the difference between expression and description, or between emotive language and cognitive language. (1953:101)

In the new configuration of ideas described by Abrams, particularity is the province of poetry, which speaks of individual experience. Universalism belongs to science, which describes nature as it is, not as idiosyncratic individuals experience it. Prose fiction, and history as well, came to lie somewhere in between poetry and science. Moreover, criticism of the novel at the time of Austen's death took a decisive turn toward realism and away from eighteenth-century concerns for the moral effects of fiction. In the 1790s, according to Litz, "most criticism of fiction still echoed Dr. Johnson's concern with the moral impact of an art-form. . . . The era of serious attention to the art of fiction did not begin until near the end of Jane Austen's lifetime; indeed, Scott's review of *Emma* . . . marks a turning-point in the criticism of the novel" (1965: 4). To speak of this historical shift as the beginning of serious criticism is, of course, to adopt a teleological view that equates being serious with modern concerns with realism. By contrast, we would argue that for the purposes of reading Austen's *Juvenilia*, it is useful to open, rather than close, the critical trajectory from Dr. Johnson to Sir Walter Scott sketched by Litz.

In a famous essay (*Rambler* no. 4, March 31, 1750) Johnson described the contemporary novel in these terms: "The works of fiction, with which the present generation seems more particularly delighted, are such as exhibit life in its true state, diversified only by accidents that daily happen in the world, and influenced by passions and qualities which are really to be found in conversing with mankind" (1806: 18). Johnson called this sort of writing "the comedy of romance" and distinguished it from "the fictions of the last age," which he styled "heroick romance." For Johnson, the earlier fiction embodied a "wild strain of imagination." It depended on "machines and expedients" and could be produced "without fear of criticism, without the toil of study, without knowledge of nature, or acquaintance with life." By contrast, the newer fictions, Johnson thought, required both book learning and "general converse and accurate observation of the living world" (18–19).

Johnson suggested that contemporary writers, writing accurately about "the living world," are the targets for a criticism based solely on mimetic criteria. Such writers "are engaged in portraits of which every one knows the original, and can detect any deviation from exactness of resemblance." Thus these writers are, according to Johnson, "in danger from every common reader." Reacting to that threat—to "the fear of not being approved as just copiers of human manners"—they have come to forget the more important question of the moral effects of their fiction upon readers (19). Johnson saw little danger to readers in the more fantastic romances of an earlier period, wherein "every transaction and sentiment was so remote from all that passes among men, that the reader was in very little danger of making any applications to himself" (20). By the same logic, however, the newer, realistic romancers must, according to Johnson, choose their objects carefully, for "when an adventurer is levelled with the rest of the world, and acts in such scenes of the universal drama, as may be the lot of any other man; young spectators fix their eyes upon him with closer attention, and hope, by observing his behaviour and success, to regulate their own practices, when they shall be engaged in the like part" (20).

Thus, Johnson continued, writers of fiction must utilize the selectivity that fiction allows to depict virtue rather than vice. Indeed, it is precisely the selectivity of fiction that makes it fit to be read by young, impressionable readers:

> The chief advantage which these fictions have over real life is, that their authors are at liberty, though not to invent, yet to select objects, and to cull from the mass of mankind, those individuals upon which the attention ought most to be employed. . . .
> It is justly considered as the greatest excellency of art, to imitate nature; but it is necessary to distinguish those parts of nature, which are most proper for imitation: greater care is still required in representing life, which is so often discoloured by passion, or deformed by wickedness. If the world be promiscuously described, I cannot see of what use it can be to read the account: or why it may not be as safe to turn the eye immediately upon mankind as upon a mirror which shows all that presents itself without discrimination. (21)

Here, then, is a critical sensibility in which moral teaching is served, rather than superseded, by mimesis. According to Johnson, realism unrefined by morality is not only promiscuous, but it collapses the distance between narrative and life, so that the former becomes a mere mirror of the latter and, as such, useless. Indeed, Johnson finds a morally neutral mimetic aesthetic to be dangerous: "It is therefore not a sufficient vindication of a . . . narrative, that the train of events is agreeable to observation and experience; for that observation which is called knowledge of the world, will be found much more frequently to make men cunning than good" (21).

Turning now to the most important of the early reviews of Austen's work, those of Walter Scott and Richard Whately, we find that mimesis begins to overshadow moral teaching in the discussion of what makes a good work of fiction. Like Johnson, Scott opposed a newer, realistic fiction to previous generations of romantic narrative. The new fiction, Scott argued, replaced the clichés of heroic romances and sentimental novels with "the art of copying from nature as she really exists in the common walks of life." Moreover, like Johnson, Scott thought that a "peculiar difficulty" faced by writers of the newer fiction was its vulnerability to "an extensive range of criticism which general experience offers to every reader" (1815: 193). Unlike Johnson, however, Scott did not dwell on the moral traps that realism can present to readers. For him, the attraction of the new realistic novel was that of recognition: "it affords to those who frequent it a pleasure nearly allied with the experience of their own social habits." By constrast, its weaknesses were two. First, an overly realistic portrayal of the mundane could bore readers. Scott criticized Austen's "characters of folly or simplicity, such as those of old Woodhouse and Miss Bates," for being "as tiresome in fiction as in real society." Second, Scott thought that a disenchanted world actually needed the extravagance of romantic fiction to teach generosity of spirit.

Scott's discussion in the *Quarterly Review* was followed six years later by that of Richard Whately in the same periodical. Like Johnson and Scott, he spoke of a progression from romance to sentimental novels to the realistic novels of a writer like Austen. But like Scott and unlike Johnson, Whately suggested that realism in and of itself is "instructive":

When this Flemish painting [i.e., the realistic novel of Austen] . . . is introduced—this accurate and unexaggerated delineation of events and characters—it necessarily follows, that a novel, which makes good its pretensions of giving a perfectly correct picture of common life, becomes a far more *instructive* work than one of equal or superior merit of the other class [sentimental novels]; it guides the judgment, and supplies a kind of artificial experience. (1821: 353)

Whately went on to argue, in accord with Johnson and Scott, that romances in which the unnatural figured could not mislead readers, whereas those that traded in the merely improbable could:

> But it is otherwise with those fictions which differ from common life in little or nothing but the improbability of the occurrences: the reader is insensibly led to calculate upon some of those lucky incidents and opportune coincidences of which he has been so much accustomed to read . . . and to feel a sort of confidence that however romantic his conduct may be, and in whatever difficulties it may involve him, all will be sure to come right at last, as is invariably the case with the hero of the novel. (354)

Here Whately complains not, as Johnson had, of the confusion of virtue and vice but of improbability as a source of miscalculation. If realistic novels supply artificial experience, then that experience had better be accurately delineated, else it will mislead readers who may take such narrated experiences to be facsimiles of real experience. As to virtue and vice, he praised Austen for precisely the psychological realism that Johnson denounced; that is, for showing the imperfections of character even of heroes and heroines (366–67).

After Scott and Whately, the dominant theme in critical discussions of Jane Austen was her realism. As Joseph Duffy puts it, summarizing nineteenth-century critical responses to Austen: "Again and again, it was her realism . . . that caught the attention and stimulated the criticism of readers" (1986: 84). Indeed, concern for the moral effects of fiction may strike us today as decidedly old-fashioned, given our education in reading texts either as representations of the real world or as linguistic objects unto themselves. In sum, we have come to presuppose separated worlds of text and life. In this view, neither writing nor reading are considered social action in the world.

Now it is just this view, and the understanding of realism that goes with it, that we wish to challenge with a rereading of the *Juvenilia*. It is surely not wrong to argue, as many critics have, that in her first works Austen was parodying the worn-out conventions of what Scott (1815: 190) called "the land of fiction," as well as readers who modeled their sentiments and actions on those found within sentimental novels. Indeed, it has been pointed out by numerous critics and biographers that the reading and criticism of contemporary literature were domestic, social activities that Austen engaged in with parents, siblings, nephews, nieces, and neighbors. Jane Austen exchanged inscribed tales and critical responses with a great many of her consociates (Chapman 1969: 431–39). This instance of literature as social activity should alert us to the possibility that an extreme separation of fiction and reality, however congenial to us today, ought not to be imposed on Jane Austen. Moreover, if we resist the impulse to dismiss the *Juvenilia* as mere childish fancy, amateurish and improbable, we can use them to rethink the relationship of writing to social life.

Let us consider the *Juvenilia* as *pensée sauvage*—as a form of social action in which a native has created alternatives to lived principles of social order. The alternatives take the form of fictions, to be sure, but these are engagements and manipulations of other fictions—the fictive rules experienced in social interactions. "Frederic & Elfrida," for instance, concerns what we have termed incest, or love (leading to marriage) between partners who are too close (patri-parallel cousins) and too much alike. The closeness of the protagonists is suggested in the title of the piece (by the similarity of their names) and is explicitly developed in the first lines:

> The Uncle of Elfrida was the Father of Frederic; in other words, they were first cousins by the Father's side.
>
> Being both born in one day & both brought up at one school, it was not wonderfull [i.e., surprising] that they should look on each other with something more than bare politeness. They loved with mutual sincerity but were both determined not to transgress the rules of Propriety by owning their attachment, either to the object beloved, or to any one else. (*MW* 4)

Here the lovers' near identity is both natural (they are born on the same day to two brothers) and social (they are raised together). Moreover, in "Frederic & Elfrida" incestuous romance occurs notwithstanding "rules of Propriety" so strict as to preclude the communication of the cousins' romantic interests. Thus, in this narration, twofold endogamous limits are violated even as we are told of conventions which, if followed, would eliminate the very possibility of transgression.[2]

As the story progresses, Elfrida's friend, Charlotte, accepts offers of marriage from two men in one afternoon—"an aged gentleman with a sallow face & old pink Coat," and "a young & Handsome Gentleman with a new blue coat" (8). She then "sat down to Supper on a young Leveret, a brace of Partridges, a leash of Pheasants & a Dozen of Pigeons" (9). Here the theme is not merely bigamy but unrestrained appetite, suggested both by Charlotte's instantaneous and successive acceptance of two men representing the range of possible exterior qualities and by the inordinate consumption of food following the inordinate consumption of men. Charlotte then commits suicide when she reflects on "the double engagement she had entered into" (9).

Charlotte's excesses can be related to other undomesticated associations that recur in the *Juvenilia*. The association of sexuality and food is repeated briefly in "Amelia Webster," as an admirer writes to his object: "I saw you thro' a telescope, & was so struck by your Charms that from that time to this I have not tasted human food" (49). Inverting Charlotte's case, here the absence of close and reciprocal communication is accompanied by an absence of food. Moreover, the specification of "human food" suggests the possibility of human consumption of animal food, and thus of the transgression of the boundary between human and animal. A related blurring of this boundary is glimpsed briefly in "Jack & Alice," where a man unmarriageable because too perfect is said to be "of so dazzling a Beauty that none but Eagles could look him in the Face" (13). Here, relations between humans and animals occur in the absence of proper social relations among humans.

These examples suggest an almost mythic dimension of the young author's thinking. To see in the earliest of the *Juvenilia* a kind

2. For other explorations of the presence of romance in the transgression of endogamous limits see Boon's discussion of Balinese patri-parallel cousin marriage (1977: 119–44).

of wild alter-cultural vision—an unrestrained probing of the limits of convention, even a mythic transcendence of the line separating nature from culture, animal from human—is to disagree with critics who have seen in them a realist's apprenticeship by way of parody, and nothing more. The *Juvenilia* are not merely improbable parodies, they are thoughtful constructions of alter-cultural possibilities. In that sense, their very improbability makes them not amateurish preludes to the realistic fictions of Austen's maturity but wilder, less subtle versions of the thoughtful play that is practiced by Austen's heroines (cf. Holly 1989: 46).

Why Jane Austen?

We have located Jane Austen in the midst of a realignment within the constellation of fiction, fact, and truth. We recognize—indeed, we insist—that this realignment has more than one history; there was no one period, and no single locus, of change. For example, Mary Campbell's *The Witness and the Other World* (1988) locates the fissure between fiction and science in the history of European writings about Asia between 400 and 1600. In Campbell's account this genre splits into fictional entertainments serving the demands of the mass market and scientific catalogs and nomenclatures serving the demands of commerce and imperialism. We would not so much disagree with Campbell's chronology as emphasize that Austen's texts show us that some two hundred years after Campbell's endpoint it was still possible, at least in Austen's domestic context, to straddle and contest the divide between fiction and nonfiction. Our hope, moreover, is that our dialogue with Austen's texts has demonstrated the possibility of contesting this divide today.

A primary goal of this book has been to open up the possibility of Austen becoming a source of alternative strategies for the narration of social realities, both exotic and familiar. In their attention to ordinary activities and persons, and to what is observable and public in human life, Austen's works are recognizably ethnographic and admirably realistic. Yet her texts depart substantially from the ethnographic realism of twentieth-century anthropology. Modern ethnographies have characteristically subscribed to a scientific realism in which language is regarded as no more than a set of labels for independently existent things. It has subscribed, in short, to a realism that would have language be a separate order from a world it serves merely to name. "No one can understand the word 'cheese,'" to quote Bertrand Russell's famous formulation of this positivism, "unless he has a nonlinguistic acquaintance with cheese" (Russell 1950: 18, cited in Jakobson 1959: 232).

Under this epistemological regime—when these conceptions of meaning and being authorize truth—fiction and nonfiction are distinct and opposed genres. Our sponsorship of fiction as a mode of ethnographic writing and ethnological comparison does not extend to the fiction of this reified world. Rather, we question both the authority of a science that nominalizes language and objectifies the world, and the chimeric liberation of a literature and criticism that regards language alone as its province. Our reading of Austen's oeuvre argues that for Austen, the world of the text and the world of the world are not separated in this way. For Austen, contra Auden, literature does make things happen. It plays with the fictive rules of social life and thereby makes visible both the contingency of all such rules and the polysemy of social action.

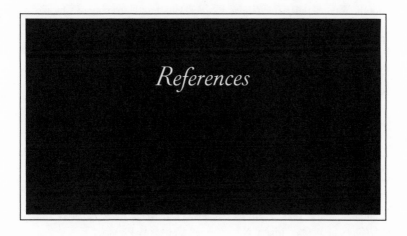

References

Abrams, M. H. 1953. *The Mirror and the Lamp: Romantic Theory and the Critical Tradition*. London: Oxford University Press.

Armstrong, Nancy. 1987. *Desire and Domestic Fiction: A Political History of the Novel*. New York: Oxford University Press.

Austen, Jane. 1932–69. *The Oxford Illustrated Jane Austen*. 3d ed., vols. 1–6. Ed. R. W. Chapman. Oxford: Oxford University Press.

Bakhtin, M. M. 1981. *The Dialogic Imagination*. Trans. C. Emerson and M. Holquist. Austin: University of Texas Press.

Bloom, Allan. 1968. "Introduction." In *Politics and the Arts: Letter to M. D'Alembert on the Theatre* [1758], by Jean-Jacques Rousseau. Trans. A. Bloom. Ithaca, N.Y.: Cornell University Press, 1968, xi–xxxiv.

Boas, Franz. 1966. *Kwakiutl Ethnography*. Ed. H. Codere. Chicago: University of Chicago Press.

Boon, James. 1977. *The Anthropological Romance of Bali 1597–1972*. Cambridge: Cambridge University Press.

———. 1982. *Other Tribes, Other Scribes: Symbolic Anthropology in the Comparative Study of Cultures, Histories, Religions, and Texts*. Cambridge: Cambridge University Press.

Boon, James, and David Schneider. 1974. "Kinship vis-à-vis Myth: Contrasts in Lévi-Strauss' Approaches to Cross-cultural Comparison." *American Anthropologist* 76:799–817.

Booth, Wayne. 1961. *The Rhetoric of Fiction.* Chicago: University of Chicago Press.

Brissenden, R. F. 1975. *"Mansfield Park*: Freedom and the Family." In *Jane Austen: Bicentenary Essays*, ed. John Halperin, 156–71. Cambridge: Cambridge University Press.

Buckley, Thomas. 1987. "Dialogue and Shared Authority: Informants as Critics." *Central Issues in Anthropology* 7(1):13–24.

Burke, Edmund. [1790] 1968. *Reflections on the Revolution in France.* New York: Penguin.

Butler, J. R. M. [1914] 1963. *The Passing of the Great Reform Bill.* London: Frank Cass.

Butler, Marilyn. 1975. *Jane Austen and the War of Ideas.* Oxford: Oxford University Press.

Campbell, Mary. 1988. *The Witness and the Other World: Exotic European Travel Writing, 400–1600.* Ithaca, N.Y.: Cornell University Press.

Chapman, R. W., ed. 1969. "Opinions of *Mansfield Park* and *Emma* c. 1815–16." In *The Oxford Illustrated Jane Austen*, ed. R. W. Chapman, 6:431–39. Oxford: Oxford University Press.

Clifford, James. 1988. *The Predicament of Culture: Twentieth-Century Ethnography, Literature, and Art.* Cambridge, Mass.: Harvard University Press.

Copeland, Edward. 1986. "Jane Austen and the Consumer Revolution." In *The Jane Austen Companion*, ed. J. David Grey, 77–92. New York: Macmillan.

Corrigan, Philip, and Derek Sayer. 1985. *The Great Arch: English State Formation as Cultural Revolution.* Oxford: Blackwell.

Cott, Nancy. 1987. *The Grounding of Modern Feminism.* New Haven, Conn.: Yale University Press.

Cottom, Daniel. 1985. *The Civilized Imagination: A Study of Ann Radcliffe, Jane Austen, and Sir Walter Scott.* New York: Cambridge University Press.

Duckworth, Alistair. 1971. *The Improvement of the Estate.* Baltimore: Johns Hopkins University Press.

Duffy, Joseph. 1986. "Criticism, 1814–70." In *The Jane Austen Companion*, ed. J. David Grey, 93–101. New York: Macmillan.

Dumont, Louis. 1970. *Homo Hierarchicus.* Trans. M. Sainsbury. Chicago: University of Chicago Press.

Errington, Shelly. 1979. "Some Comments on Style in the Meaning of the Past." *Journal of Asian Studies* 38(2):231–44.

Evans-Pritchard, E. E. 1932. "Heredity and Gestation as the Azande See Them." In *Social Anthropology and Other Essays.* New York: Free Press, 1962, 243–56.

——. 1933. "Zande Blood-Brotherhood." In *Social Anthropology and Other Essays.* New York: Free Press, 1962, 257–87.

——. 1936. "Zande Theology." In *Social Anthropology and Other Essays.* New York: Free Press, 1962, 288–329.

——. 1937. *Witchcraft, Oracles, and Magic among the Azande.* Oxford: Oxford University Press.

——. 1962. *Social Anthropology and Other Essays.* New York: Free Press.

——. 1976. "Some Reminiscences and Reflections on Fieldwork." In *Witchcraft, Oracles, and Magic among the Azande.* Abridged ed. Oxford: Oxford University Press, 240–56.

Favret-Saada, Jeanne. 1980. *Deadly Words: Witchcraft in the Bocage.* Trans. C. Cullen. Cambridge: Cambridge University Press.

García Márquez, Gabriel. 1983. "The Solitude of Latin America." Nobel Prize address, reproduced in *Chicago Tribune,* March 6, 1983, sec. 2, p. 4.

Geertz, Clifford. 1973. *The Interpretation of Cultures.* New York: Basic Books.

Grey, J. David, ed. 1986. *The Jane Austen Companion.* New York: Macmillan.

Halperin, John. 1984. *The Life of Jane Austen.* Baltimore: Johns Hopkins University Press.

Handler, Richard. 1985. "On Dialogue and Destructive Analysis: Problems in Narrating Nationalism and Ethnicity." *Journal of Anthropological Research* 41:171–82.

——. 1988. *Nationalism and the Politics of Culture in Quebec.* Madison: University of Wisconsin Press.

Harding, D. W. 1940. "Regulated Hatred: An Aspect of the Work of Jane Austen." In *Critics on Jane Austen,* ed. Judith O'Neill, 42–49. Coral Gables, Fla.: University of Miami Press, 1970.

Harris, Wilson. 1970. "History, Fable, and Myth in the Caribbean and the Guianas." *Caribbean Quarterly* 16(2):1–32.

Holly, Grant. 1989. "*Emma*grammatology." In *Studies in Eighteenth-Century Culture,* ed. L. E. Brown and P. Craddock, 39–51. East Lansing, Mich.: Colleagues Press.

Jakobson, Roman. 1959. "On Linguistic Aspects of Translation." In *On Translation,* ed. Reuben Brower, 232–39. Cambridge, Mass.: Harvard University Press.

Johnson, Claudia L. 1988. *Jane Austen: Women, Politics, and the Novel.* Chicago: University of Chicago Press.

Johnson, Samuel. 1806. *The Rambler.* 16th ed. London: Joyce Gold.

Keesing, R. M. 1985. "Conventional Metaphors and Anthropological Metaphysics: The Problematic of Cultural Translation." *Journal of Anthropological Research* 41:201–17.

Kirkham, Margaret. 1983. *Jane Austen, Feminism, and Fiction.* Totowa, N.J.: Barnes and Noble.

Kroeber, A. L., and Clyde Kluckhohn. 1963. *Culture: A Critical Review of Concepts and Definitions.* New York: Vintage Books.

Lévi-Strauss, Claude. [1949] 1969. *The Elementary Structures of Kinship.* Rev. ed. Trans. J. von Sturmer and R. Needham. Boston: Beacon Press.

Litz, A. Walton. 1965. *Jane Austen: A Study of Her Artistic Development.* New York: Oxford University Press.

Macfarlane, Alan. 1978. *The Origins of English Individualism.* Oxford: Blackwell.

———. 1986. *Marriage and Love in England 1300–1840.* Oxford: Blackwell.

Macpherson, C. B. 1962. *The Political Theory of Possessive Individualism.* Oxford: Oxford University Press.

Mansell, Darrel. 1973. *The Novels of Jane Austen: An Interpretation.* London: Macmillan.

Marcus, George, and Michael Fischer. 1986. *Anthropology as Cultural Critique.* Chicago: University of Chicago Press.

Marshall, David. 1986. "Rousseau and the State of Theater." *Representations* 13:84–114.

Mead, Margaret. [1935] 1963. *Sex and Temperament in Three Primitive Societies.* New York: Dell.

Miller, D. A. 1981. *Narrative and Its Discontents: Problems of Closure in the Traditional Novel.* Princeton, N.J.: Princeton University Press.

Mingay, G. E. 1963. *English Landed Society in the Eighteenth Century.* London: Routledge and Kegan Paul.

Morgan, Susan, and Susan Kneedler. 1989. "Austen's Sexual Politics." Paper presented at the annual meeting of the Modern Language Association, Washington, D.C.

Morrill, J. S. 1979. "The Northern Gentry and the Great Rebellion." *Northern History* 20:66–87.

Mudrick, Marvin. 1952. *Jane Austen: Irony as Defense and Discovery.* Princeton, N.J.: Princeton University Press.

Newton, Judith Lowder. 1981. *Women, Power, and Subversion: Social Strategies in British Fiction, 1778–1860.* Athens: University of Georgia Press.

O'Boyle, Lenore. 1979. "The Classless Society: Comment on Stearns." *Comparative Studies in Society and History* 21:397–413.

Phillips, K. C. 1970. *Jane Austen's English.* London: Deutsch.

Poovey, Mary. 1984. *The Proper Lady and the Woman Writer.* Chicago: University of Chicago Press.

Rousseau, Jean-Jacques. [1758] 1968. *Politics and the Arts: Letter to M.*

D'Alembert on the Theatre. Trans. A. Bloom. Ithaca, N.Y.: Cornell University Press.

———. [1755] 1973. *The Social Contract and Discourses*. Trans. G. D. H. Cole. New York: Dutton.

Russell, Bertrand. 1950. "Logical Positivism." *Revue Internationale de Philosophie* 4(1)3–19.

Sapir, Edward. 1949. *Selected Writings of Edward Sapir*. Ed. D. G. Mandelbaum. Berkeley: University of California Press.

Schneider, David M. 1968. *American Kinship: A Cultural Account*. Englewood Cliffs, N.J.: Prentice-Hall.

Schorer, Mark. 1952. "Fiction and the 'Analogical Matrix.'" In *Critiques and Essays on Modern Fiction*, ed. John Aldridge, 83–98. New York: Ronald Press.

Scott, Sir Walter. 1815. "Emma; a Novel." *Quarterly Review* 14:188–201.

Segal, Daniel. 1988. "Nationalism, Comparatively Speaking." *Journal of Historical Sociology* 1(3):300–321.

Shrage, Laurie. 1989. "Should Feminists Oppose Prostitution?" *Ethics* 99:347–61.

Simpson, Richard. [1870] 1968. Unsigned review of *Memoir of Jane Austen*, by J. E. Austen-Leigh. In *Jane Austen: The Critical Heritage*, ed. B. Southam, 241–65. London: Routledge and Kegan Paul.

Southam, Brian. 1986a. "*Persuasion*: The Canceled Chapters." In *The Jane Austen Companion*, ed. J. David Grey, 322–23. New York: Macmillan.

———. 1986b. "*Juvenilia*." In *The Jane Austen Companion*, ed. J. David Grey, 244–55. New York: Macmillan.

Spring, David. 1963. "Aristocracy, Social Structure, and Religion in the Early Victorian Period." *Victorian Studies* 6:263–80.

———. 1983. "Interpreters of Jane Austen's Social World: Literary Critics and Historians." In *Jane Austen: New Perspectives*, ed. Janet Todd, 53–72. New York: Holmes and Meier.

Stern, G. B. 1944. *Speaking of Jane Austen*. New York: Harper.

Stocking, George W., Jr. 1983a. "The Ethnographer's Magic: Fieldwork in British Anthropology from Tylor to Malinowski." *History of Anthropology* 1:70–120.

———. 1983b. "The 'Genesis' of Anthropology: The Discipline's First Paradigm." Distinguished Lecture, Fifty-ninth Annual Meeting of the Central States Anthropological Society, April 8, 1983.

Strathern, Marilyn. 1989. *After Nature: English Kinship in the Late Twentieth Century*. The Morgan Lectures, University of Rochester.

Swingle, L. J. 1979. "The Poets, the Novelists, and the English Romantic Situation." *The Wordsworth Circle* 10(2):118–28.

Tanner, Tony. 1986. *Jane Austen*. London: Macmillan.

Taussig, Michael. 1980. *The Devil and Commodity Fetishism in South America*. Chapel Hill: University of North Carolina Press.

Tave, Stuart. 1973. *Some Words of Jane Austen*. Chicago: University of Chicago Press.

Thompson, F. M. L. 1963. *English Landed Society in the Nineteenth Century*. London: Routledge and Kegan Paul.

Trilling, Lionel. 1955. *The Opposing Self*. New York: Harcourt.

Van Ghent, Dorothy. 1953. *The English Novel: Form and Function*. New York: Rinehart.

Whately, Archbishop Richard. 1821. "Northanger Abbey, and Persuasion." *Quarterly Review* 21:352–76.

Wollstonecraft, Mary. [1790] 1960. *A Vindication of the Rights of Men*. Gainesville, Fla.: Scholars' Facsimiles and Reprints.

———. [1792] 1967. *A Vindication of the Rights of Woman*. New York: Norton.

Index

ABOUT THE AUTHORS

Richard Handler studied English literature at Columbia University and in 1979 received his Ph.D. in anthropology from the University of Chicago. He is the author of *Nationalism and the Politics of Culture in Quebec*, published in 1988, and of numerous essays on the literary and cultural criticism of American anthropologists during the first half of the twentieth century. Since 1986, he has been a faculty member of the Department of Anthropology at the University of Virginia.

Daniel Segal received his B.A. from Cornell University (1980) and his Ph.D. in anthropology from the University of Chicago (1989) for a study of nationalism, social stratification, and state formation in Trinidad and Tobago. He has also conducted field research on American medical education. Reports on his research have appeared in numerous professional journals, and he has curated an exhibition of Caribbean visual arts. Since 1986, he has taught anthropology at Pitzer College of the Claremont Colleges.